Smith Wigglesworth
APOSTLE OF FAITH

STANLEY HOWARD FRODSHAM

GOSPEL PUBLISHING HOUSE
Springfield, MO 65802-1894
02-0586

15th Printing 1997

International Standard Book Number 0-88243-586-8
Printed in the United States of America

CONTENTS

FOREWORD

Dedicated Christians say it in different ways: Above all else, they wish that during their lifetime their words and examples might nudge others toward the Savior, that others might discover the forgiveness, joy, and peace they did.

The ultimate hope of such Christians is that even after death they would continue bearing fruit, through either their converts or their writings.

Smith Wigglesworth—one of the best-known Pentecostal evangelists of the early 20th century—lived with these noble goals. He was always ready to nudge others toward the Savior and faith in the Word of God. Some would even say his nudges were more like shoves, so intent was he on having people believe in the Lord.

Be that as it may, his biography continues in print more than 40 years after his death, indicating this generation has a high regard for Wigglesworth's inspiring life of faith. Other books written about him in recent years only attest to this regard.

Good historians are more than couriers of the past. They search out apparently dull facts most of us would overlook. Working like a detective, they analyze information and come to conclusions about their subject. That is the way Stanley H. Frodsham looked at the life of his dear friend Smith Wigglesworth. The result is an inspiring and insightful biography, a classic rags-to-riches (in faith) story.

Wigglesworth's first 48 years were anything but world-shaking. He was a plumber. He could hardly read until after he married and his wife began to tutor him. True, he was personable and had a reputation as an aggressive witness for Christ. And he helped in a local mission. But his wife did the preaching.

There is one thing that might have indicated Smith Wigglesworth would someday be known beyond his Bradford, England. One thing did suggest he might command the attention of audiences in faraway Australia, South Africa, and North America. When he prayed for people who were ill or diseased, they got healed.

Even so, his vocation-changing experience did not come until he was baptized in the Holy Spirit under the ministry of Anglican leaders, Alexander and Mary Boddy.

For the next 40 years his name was linked with salvation-healing meetings around the world. His ministry boosted churches and affected entire regions for the Kingdom. The former plumber of Bradford, England, became known as the Apostle of Faith.

Now, more than a generation after his death, Smith Wigglesworth continues to bless and inspire believers. Through books such as this, he is still nudging—or shoving—people toward the Savior and faith in God's Word. He was that kind of Christian.

WAYNE WARNER, DIRECTOR
ASSEMBLIES OF GOD ARCHIVES

ACKNOWLEDGMENT AND TRIBUTE

SMITH WIGGLESWORTH constantly acknowledged how much he owed under God to a wonderful wife, but he was also equally grateful for a remarkable daughter. We first visited his home in 1909 when Alice Wigglesworth was spending her first term in Africa. The constant theme of his conversation from morning until night was "our Alice."

After the home going of Mrs. Wigglesworth in 1913, Alice Wigglesworth—who was later married to James Salter—in large manner took the place of her mother, traveling constantly with her father in his many journeys to different countries. Especially was this so during the last years of his life. Mrs. Salter herself had an inspiring ministry like her mother's, and Mr. Wigglesworth encouraged her constantly to stir up the saints with her fiery message before he himself gave forth the Word.

Again and again James Salter unselfishly returned to his missionary labors in the Belgian Congo alone, because he knew how much Smith Wigglesworth appreciated the companionship of his daughter Alice. Mr. Salter also made many trips with his father-in-law, relieving him of all business matters and supplementing the Wigglesworth campaigns with his own unique and inspiring missionary messages.

Smith Wigglesworth owed more than we can ever estimate to these two loyal helpers, and incidentally, this book owes its existence to the large amount of information they have supplied. They really should have written this volume themselves, but they insisted that another should have the credit for producing it. The one who is named as author, who edited the material supplied, desires to acknowledge the fact that the credit for the contents of this book rightfully belongs to his friends— JAMES AND ALICE SALTER.

STANLEY HOWARD FRODSHAM

Springfield, Mo., U.S.A.

I

"FIRST THE BLADE"

~~~~~~

THE YEAR 1859 is known as that of the great Irish revival. Two years previously, a mighty awakening had come to America. Prayer meetings had been held in every large city, and were attended by thousands of people. As men called on God, the Spirit of the Lord mightily worked, and it was estimated that every month fifty thousand souls were converted. The news of the revival of 1857 in the U.S.A. and of the revival of 1859 in Ireland, set the people of Britain to praying. Soon revival fires began to burn throughout that country. Spurgeon preached to vast throngs in London and at every service many received Jesus Christ as their Savior and Lord.

In Wales, Christmas Evans was engaged in a wonderful evangelistic ministry. His converts became so exuberantly happy that they would dance for joy in his meetings, and Evans would not restrain them. Because of this, scores of sinners sought Christ in order to receive the same "joy unspeakable." At the same time, the hearts of many who were attending the Wesleyan

9

Methodist churches throughout Great Britain were "strangely warmed." One of their evangelists, William Booth, was singularly used. In 1859 he broke with the Wesleyan church to give himself entirely to the work of evangelism and was led to choose the slums of the east end of London as his first place of ministry. The worst of sinners were transformed into the greatest of saints and went preaching the gospel throughout the land. Booth later founded the Salvation Army.

It was in this revival year of 1859, in a humble shack in Menston, in Yorkshire, England, that Smith Wigglesworth was born. One day when he was holding a meeting in Riverside, California, we said to him: "Tell us your story." He related to us the following:

Wigglesworth Tells of Early Life

My father was very poor and worked long hours for little pay in order to support Mother and us three boys and one girl. I can remember one cold frosty day when my father had been given the job of digging a ditch seven yards long and a yard deep, and filling it up again, for the sum of three shillings and six pence (about eighty-seven cents). My mother said that if he would only wait a bit, it might thaw and his task would be easier. But he needed that money for food, for there was none in the house. So he set to work with a pickaxe. The frost was a full yard deep, but underneath the hard ground was some soft wet clay. As he threw up some of this, a robin suddenly appeared, picked up a worm, ate it, flew to a branch of a nearby tree, and from there sent out a song of joyous praise. Up to now, Father had been very despondent, but he was so entranced by the robin's lovely song of thanksgiving that he took fresh courage and began to dig with renewed vigor—saying to himself, "If that robin can sing like that for a worm, surely I can work like a father for my good wife and my four fine children!"

When I was six years of age, I got work in the field, pulling and cleaning turnips, and I can remember how sore my tiny hands became pulling turnips from morning until night.

At seven years of age, my older brother and I went to work in a woolen mill. My father obtained employment in the same mill as a weaver. Things were easier in our house from that time on, and food became more plentiful.

My father was a great lover of birds and at one time he had sixteen song birds in our home. Like my father I had a great love for birds and at every opportunity I would be out looking for their nests. I always knew where there were some eighty or ninety of them. One time I found a nest full of fledglings, and thinking they were abandoned, I adopted them, taking them home and making a place for them in my bedroom. Somehow the parent birds discovered them and would fly in through the open window and feed their young ones. One time I had both a thrush and a lark feeding their young ones in my room. My brothers and I would catch some songbirds by means of birdlime, bring them home, and later sell them in the market.

My mother was very industrious with her needle and made all our clothes, chiefly from old garments that had been given to her. I usually wore an overcoat with sleeves three or four inches too long, which was very comfortable in cold weather. I cannot forget those long winter nights and mornings, having to get out of bed at five o'clock to snatch a quick meal and then walk two miles to be at work by six. We had to work twelve hours each day, and I often said to my father, "It's a long time from six until six in the mill." I can remember the tears in his eyes as he said: "Well, six o'clock will always come." Sometimes it seemed like a month coming.

I can never recollect a time when I did not long for God. Even though neither Father nor Mother knew God, I was always seeking Him. I would often kneel down in the field and ask Him to help me. I would ask

Him especially to enable me to find where the birds' nests were, and after I had prayed I seemed to have an instinct to know exactly where to look.

One time I walked to work in a great thunderstorm. It seemed that for half an hour I was enveloped with fire as the thunders rolled and the lightnings flashed. Young as I was, my heart was crying to God for His preservation, and He wrapped me in His gracious presence. Though all the way I was surrounded with lightning and I was drenched to the skin, I knew no fear—I only sensed that I was being shielded by the power of God.

My grandmother was an old-time Wesleyan Methodist and would take me to the meetings she attended. When I was eight years of age there was a revival meeting held in her church. I can remember one Sunday morning at seven o'clock when all those simple folks were dancing around a big stove in the center of the church, clapping their hands and singing:

> Oh, the Lamb, the bleeding Lamb,
> The Lamb of Calvary,
> The Lamb that was slain,
> That liveth again
> To intercede for me.

As I clapped my hands and sang with them, a clear knowledge of the new birth came into my soul. I looked to the Lamb of Calvary. I believed that He loved me and had died for me. Life came in—eternal life—and I knew that I had received a new life which had come from God. I was born again. I saw that God wants us so badly that He has made the condition as simple as He possibly could—"Only believe." That experience was real and I have never doubted my salvation since that day.

But I had no words. The longer I lived the more I thought, but the less language I had to express my thoughts. In this respect I resembled my mother. She would begin to tell a story, but what she said was so unintelligible that Father would have to interrupt, saying, "Nay, Mother, you'll have to begin again!" She just could not express herself. I was the same.

But I delighted in going to meetings, especially those in which everyone was giving a testimony. I would arise to give mine, but would have no language to convey what I felt in the depths of my soul. Invariably I would burst out crying. One memorable day three old men, whom I knew very intimately, came across to where I was weeping, unable to speak. They laid their hands on me. The Spirit of the Lord came upon me and I was instantly set free from my bondage. I not only believed, but I could also speak.

From the time of my conversion I became a soul winner, and the first person I won for Christ was my own dear mother.

When I was nine years of age I was tall, and so I got full-time work in the mill. School was not compulsory in those days, and so I was robbed of an education.

Father wanted all of us to go to the Episcopal church. He had no desire to go himself, but he liked the parson, because they met at the same "pub" and drank beer together. My brother and I were in the choir in this church, and although I could not read I soon learned the tunes of the hymns and chants. When most of the boys in the choir were twelve years of age they had to be confirmed by the bishop. I was not twelve, but between nine and ten, when the bishop laid his hands on me. I can remember that as he imposed his hands I had a similar experience to the one I had forty years later when I was baptized in the Holy Spirit. My whole body was filled with the consciousness of God's presence, a consciousness that remained with me for days. After the confirmation service all the other boys were swearing and quarrelling, and I wondered what had made the difference between them and me.

When I was thirteen, we moved to Bradford. There I went to the Wesleyan Methodist church and began to enter into a deeper spiritual life. I was very keen for God. This church was having some special missionary meetings and they chose seven boys to speak. I was one of the seven chosen, and I had three weeks in which to get ready for a fifteen-minute talk. For three weeks I lived in prayer. I remember that as I began there were such loud amens and shoutings. I do not recollect what I said, but I know I was possessed with a mighty zeal, a burning desire to get people to know my Savior. At that time I was always getting in touch with boys and talking to them about salvation. I had many rebuffs and rebukes. I wanted to share the great joy I had, but so many did not seem too eager to listen to me, and that was a great mystery to me. I suppose I was not very tactful. I always carried a New Testament with me even though I was not able to read much.

When I was sixteen years of age the Salvation Army opened up a work in Bradford. I delighted to be with these earnest Salvation Army people. It was laid very deeply upon me to fast and pray for the salvation of souls in those days, and every week we saw scores of sinners yielding their hearts to Christ.

In the mill where I worked there was a godly man belonging to the Plymouth Brethren. He was a steam fitter. I was given to him as a helper and he taught me how to do plumbing work. He talked to me about water baptism and its meaning. I can remember that he said to me, "If you will obey the Lord in this, He may have something great for you." I gladly obeyed the Word of the Lord to be buried with Him in baptism unto death and come forth from that symbolic watery grave to a newness of life in God. I was about seventeen at that time.

It was this good man who taught me about the Second Coming of the Lord Jesus. Again and again when I had a sense that I had failed God, I would be troubled with the thought that the Lord would come and I would not be ready to meet Him. From time to time it was a relief to me to go to work and find this godly man there.

Then I knew the Lord had not come in the night and left me behind.

I continued with the Salvation Army because it seemed to me they had more power in their ministry than anybody else at that time. We used to have all nights of prayer. Many would be prostrated under the power of the Spirit, sometimes for as long as twenty-four hours at a time. We called that the baptism in the Spirit in those days. Those early Salvationists had great power and it was manifested in their testimony and in their lives. We would join together and claim in faith fifty or a hundred souls every week and know that we would get them. Alas, today many are not laying themselves out for soul winning but for fleshly manifestations.

I looked to the Lord, and He surely helped me in everything. When I was eighteen years of age, I went to a plumber to ask for employment. I cleaned up my shoes with an extra shine, put on a clean collar, and applied at the home of this man. He said, "No, I don't need anyone." I said, "Thank you, sir. I am sorry." The man let me walk down to his gate and then called me back, saying: "There's something about you that is different. I just can't let you go."

He sent me to do a job fitting a row of homes with water piping, which I finished in a week. The master was so amazed that he said, "It cannot possibly be done!" but he went and found the work perfect. He said he could not keep me employed at that speed.

When I was twenty years of age, I moved to Liverpool, and the power of God was mightily upon me. I had a great desire to help the young people. Every week I used to gather around me scores of boys and girls, barefooted, ragged, and hungry. I earned good money, but I spent all of it on food for those children. They would congregate in the sheds in the docks, and what meetings we had! Hundreds of them were saved. A friend of mine and I devoted ourselves to visiting the hospitals and also the ships. God gave me a great heart for the poor. I used to work hard and spend all I had on the poor and have nothing for myself. I fasted all day every Sunday and prayed, and I never remember seeing less than fifty souls saved by the power of God in the meetings with the children, in the hospitals, on the ships, and in the Salvation Army. These were the days of great soul awakening.

At the Salvation Army meetings the officer in charge would constantly ask me to speak. I cannot tell why he should ask me, for my speech was always broken, weeping before the people. I could not hold back the tears. I would have given a world to be able to speak in a more eloquent way; but like Jeremiah I was a man with a fountain of tears. But as I wept before the people, this often would lead to an altar call. I thank God for those days because the Lord kept me in a broken, contrite spirit. The memory of those Liverpool days is very precious to me.

When I was about twenty-three years of age, I was led to go back to Bradford, and I was strongly led to open up a business for myself as a plumber and give my spare time to helping the Salvation Army. It was there I met the best girl in the world!

II

"AN HELPMEET FOR HIM"

IN THE second part of the Pilgrim's Progress, Bunyan introduces us to one, Mr. Greatheart, who guided and guarded Christiana and her sons on their way to the Celestial City. The one whose story we are telling was a Mr. Greatheart. He surely had a great heart of love and loyalty to his Master, for so often we have heard him say, "Isn't He a lovely Jesus!" And he also had a great heart of love for all his fellow pilgrims, especially the poor and needy, the sick and the suffering.

He once said to us, "All that I am today I owe, under God, to my precious wife. Oh, she was lovely!"

Mary Jane Featherstone, whom God chose to be "an helpmeet for him," came from a good Methodist family. Her father was a temperance lecturer. He was heir to a large inheritance that had been made through liquor selling, but he had a conviction that filthy lucre secured through the damnation of souls would do him no good, and so he refused to touch a single penny of this tainted money. His daughter followed her father's principles of righteousness and holiness, and was always fearless in speaking her inner convictions.

When about seventeen years of age, Mary Jane, or Polly as she was often called, was placed in a milliner's store to learn the art of trimming hats and bonnets. This kind of work seemed too petty for her, so after a month of it, she decided to run away from her native town and all the restraints of home, to seek fame and fortune in Bradford. But the Lord was watching over this hand-maid to preserve her from evil.

Polly accepted service in a large family in one of the big homes in Bradford. One night she was in the center of the city and was attracted, by the sound of trumpets and the beating of drums, to a meeting held in the open air. The Salvation Army was an entirely new thing in those days, and she looked at these people with great interest. When their open-air meeting was over, they marched down the streets of Bradford. She thought to herself, "Where are these silly people, who play as they march, going?" She followed them to a dilapidated the-ater building. Dare she go into a theater? At home she had been taught that such a place was unspeakably evil. But she was inquisitive. Looking this way and that way to see if anybody who knew her was watching, she slipped in and found a seat at the top of the gallery.

The service began and her interest deepened as she listened to the bright singing and the lively witnessing of recent converts. The evangelist that night was Gipsy Tillie Smith, a sister of the famous Gipsy Rodney Smith, who also was a Salvation Army evangelist in those early days. The evangelist preached Christ with great power. The young girl in the gallery yearned to know Him and the power of His cleansing blood to wash away her sins. When the call was made for sinners to come and seek the Savior, Polly made her way from the top gallery to the penitent form (Salvation Army altar rail). At first she asked to be left alone as she called to the Lord to forgive her sins. Later, Tillie Smith knelt by her side and led her to a saving knowledge of the Lord Jesus Christ. When the assurance came that she was forgiven of all her sins, she jumped to her feet, threw her gloves in the air, and shouted, "Hallelujah, it is done!"

Smith Wigglesworth, then a young man, was in the audience. He watched that young woman pray through to God and he heard her shout "Hallelujah!" Later he declared, "It seemed as if the inspiration of God was upon her from the very first." She was a beautiful girl, and as he looked at her in her simple dress and her shapely early Victorian bonnet, he thought she was lovely. He felt the first time he heard her give her testimony that she belonged to him, and soon there began an intimate friendship between Polly Featherstone and Smith. The new convert was vivacious and soon began to make large and rapid spiritual strides. Her association with Tillie Smith and her brother Rodney and Brother Lawley—who later became a commissioner in the Salvation Army—brought her into contact with General Booth, who gave her a commission in his organization without her having to undergo the usual period of training.

Our young Greatheart had been greatly attracted to the Army because of their splendid soul-saving ministry; so he threw himself wholeheartedly into the work of the Salvationists. In it he found an outlet for the consuming passion for the unsaved, and he had a joyous satisfaction in watching the lives of many men and women change by the power of the gospel. And then Polly's presence in the meetings was a great attraction to him! Her alertness and ability in the indoor services as well as in the open-air meetings appealed to him. The officers of the Salvation Army soon recognized that there was coming a "something" between these two. It was contrary to Army rules that an officer, for they had made her such, should associate with just an ordinary "soldier," as they accounted our Greatheart (although he never actually became a member of the Salvation Army).

One day a major in the Army drove to the home where she was working and asked if she would go with him to Leith in Scotland to help start a new work. She agreed, packed her suitcase, went off to the railroad station with the major, and in a few hours she was in Scotland.

In those early days of the Salvation Army the public was very generous in contributions of over-ripe eggs and stale vegetables, and the Salvation Army lassies had to be alert to dodge these missiles. One day Polly received a black eye from an orange that was donated somewhat suddenly. But none of these things moved her. She had a lovely voice and would sing and testify in the open air. Many a window and door in the nearby flats would be flung open to hear the songs and the messages of these fearless young Salvationists. And their labors were not in vain; they were greatly blessed of God in spiritual and social service.

While in Leith, Polly took a special interest in the well-being of a recent convert who lived on the sixth floor of a tenement house, and whose husband, who was somewhat of a brute, opposed her attendance at the meetings. Finding Polly praying with his wife one day when he returned from his work, he threatened, if she did not stop praying, to forcibly eject her. She continued to pray, and so he picked her up in his arms and carried her down the five flights of steps. Every step he took, she prayed, "Lord, save this man; save his soul, Lord." The man swore wildly and fumed terribly, but she had the joy of hearing him cry for mercy when he got to the last flight. Together they knelt, and made a "penitent form" of the bottom step, where she pointed him to the Lamb of God whose blood cleanses from all sin.

One day in Leith she was brought before her superior officers who put to her certain leading questions relative to her attitude toward the opposite sex, they assuming that she had an interest in a local soldier. When they could obtain no satisfaction from her they suggested that they all kneel and she should lead in a word of prayer. She began her prayer, "Lord, you know these men think I am interested in a Scotchman! Lord, you know I am not; for if what these Scotch folk say about each other is true, they are all so stingy that they would nip a currant in two to save the other half. You know I don't believe that, Lord, about these Scotch folks, for I have found them to be very kind; but you know, Lord, I do not intend to marry anyone away up here in Scotland." She continued in this vein and by the time she got through, her examiners were ready to close the interview. Polly knew there was a young man in Bradford who was desperately in love with her, and she loved him.

She returned to that town, severing her connection with the Salvation Army and associating with a new and, in the estimation of some people, more spiritual group, which was called the Blue Ribbon Army. Mrs. Elizabeth Baxter, a very spiritual woman, was at the head of it. But Polly remained a true friend of the Salvation Army, often entertaining their officers. At that time evangelistic calls came from many Methodist churches. The Spirit of God moved mightily on her ministry and many souls were won for Christ.

When Polly was twenty-two years of age she was married to our Greatheart who was then twenty-three. In later years he paid her this tribute: "She became a great help to me in my spiritual life. She was always such an inspiration to holiness. She saw how ignorant I was, and immediately began to teach me to read properly and to write; unfortunately she never succeeded in teaching me to spell."

Speaking concerning his wife, our Greatheart testified: "She was a great soul winner. I encouraged her to continue her ministry of evangelizing, and I continued my business as a plumber. I had a burden for the parts of Bradford that had no church, and we opened up a work in a small building that I rented. As the children came we always prayed through for them before they were born, that they would belong to God. I used to carry the children to meeting and look after them while she preached. I was no preacher myself, but I was always down at the penitent form to lead souls to Christ. Her work was to put down the net, mine to land the fish. This latter is just as important as the former."

There came to Bradford a very severe winter and plumbers were in great demand. It was not only through the winter period but for the two years that followed that they were having to repair fallen spouts and other damage done by the storms. Wigglesworth and the two men who were helping him were kept busy from morning till night. In those days of much business and prosperity, his attendance at religious services declined, and his heart began to grow cold toward God; but the colder he became, the hotter his wife became for God. Her evangelistic zeal never abated, nor her prayer life. Her quiet, consistent Christian life and witness made his laxity all the more apparent, and it irritated him. One night a climax came. She was a little later than usual in getting home from the service and when she entered the house, he remarked: "I am the master of this house, and I am not going to have you coming home at so late an hour as this!" Polly quietly replied, "I know that you are my husband, but Christ is my Master." This annoyed him and he put her out the back door. But there was one thing he had forgotten to do—to lock the front door. She went around the house and came in at the front door laughing. She laughed so much that he had to laugh with her; and so that episode was finished.

When some husbands backslide, their wives get sour and nag at them from morning till night, but that was not the way of Polly Wigglesworth. She had a merry heart, and while she was on fire for the Lord, she made every mealtime a season of fun and humor. And she wooed her husband back to the Lord and to his oldtime love and zeal for God. Her fidelity was severely tested during those months when he was spiritually unsettled, but it was her gracious stability that guided him through the dangerous period, saving him from a terrible spiritual shipwreck.

Polly Wigglesworth's reputation as a winner of souls went far and wide, and not infrequently she would be sent to restore a work that was failing and to follow on in evangelistic services where others had failed. She was a popular preacher for women's services and quite a favorite with men's Bible classes. Untiring in zeal, she literally ate up work of all kinds, including the care of a large house. She and her husband were always given to hospitality, and she never complained no matter whom he brought home suddenly for a meal or invited to stay for a few days in their home. At convention times there were always large numbers entertained in her home, but never once did she murmur.

Wigglesworth had to go into Leeds one day each week to purchase plumbing supplies. In this town he found a place where there was a divine healing meeting. There was such a note of reality in these divine healing meetings and the Lord was so graciously healing people that he began to search for sick people in Bradford. He would pay their way to Leeds where the prayer of faith was offered for them. At first he said nothing to Mrs. Wigglesworth about this, for he was not sure of her reaction to this "fanaticism," as most people dubbed divine healing in those days. But she found out what he was doing and since she herself had need of healing she accompanied him one day to Leeds. There the prayer of faith was offered for her and she was healed by the Lord. From that time forward she was as ardent for the truth of the Lord's healing as he was.

The work in Bradford grew, and so they had to move to larger and yet larger premises until they settled in quite a large building in Bowland Street. In this Bowland Street Mission they had a huge text painted as a scroll on the wall back of the pulpit that everyone could see: "I am the Lord that healeth thee." In the course of years many testified to being healed through the inspiration of that verse from the Bible.

There came to this mission a brother who had a gracious ministry of healing. When the Sunday afternoon service was over, he was invited to the Wigglesworth home for tea. During the simple meal, Mrs. Wigglesworth put the question to this minister: "What would you think of a man who preaches divine healing to others, yet he himself uses medical means every day in his life?"

"I should say that that man did not fully trust the Lord," was the answer. After the meal Wigglesworth said to this minister: "When my wife was talking about one who preached divine healing to others and yet used other means himself, she was referring to me. From childhood I have suffered from hemorrhoids and so I deem it necessary to use salts every day. I have looked upon them as harmless, natural means; for I knew that if I did not have something of this kind, I should have bleeding every day, and infection might result. But if you will stand with me in faith, I am willing to trust God in this matter and give up the salts. Since I have taken them every day for years, my system is so used to them that there will be no natural function from now until Wednesday. Will you stand with me in faith on that day? for in the natural I shall have great pain and much bleeding through not having used the salts." The brother agreed.

After that Sunday Wigglesworth did not take his daily dose of salts. On Wednesday the crisis came. At a certain hour he went into his bathroom. He anointed himself with oil according to James 5. We have often heard him testify in public, for he was a man of no unwholesome modesty when it came to speaking about perfectly natural things: "God undertook. My bowels functioned that day like a baby's. God had perfectly healed me. From that day forward my bowels have functioned perfectly without the use of any means whatsoever. I have proved the God who is enough."

Polly Wigglesworth loved her husband enough to reprove him when he was wrong—and this was very often. Most husbands bitterly resent any criticism from their wives, but Wigglesworth always took her rebukes with a smile. His attitude was that of David who said, "Let the righteous smite me in kindness and correct me; oil so choice let not my head refuse." Psalm 141:5, Masoretic Rendering. Even though at times he did not take full heed to her correction, yet there is no doubt that as a whole her admonitions had a great effect in the training of her husband's character.

In his plumbing work Wigglesworth obtained a good deal of profitable business from saloonkeepers, who sent for him to repair the pumps by which they drew up the beer from their cellars. This was an abomination to Polly who in those days kept the books. She knew that the workmen would be given free drinks in the saloons, and she knew it would have a demoralizing effect on them. She prevailed in her protests, and after awhile her husband, to protect the men who were laboring for him, refused all work from saloonkeepers. This meant heavy financial losses to him, but he gave it up as a matter of principle.

We read in Psalm 127: "Children are an heritage of the Lord." The Lord gave to the Wigglesworth home five children: one girl, Alice; and four boys, Seth, Harold, Ernest, and George. George went to be with the Lord in 1915, and how greatly his loving father missed him.

III

"THEN THE EAR"

~~~~~~

MY SOUL followeth hard after Thee" (Psalm 63:8) is the intense expression of the man after God's own heart. This was ever the attitude of Smith Wigglesworth from the early days of his Christian experience. No wonder the enemy of souls sought so hard to cause the cares of this life and the deceitfulness of riches to choke the Word in the two years mentioned in the last chapter.

Bunyan's pilgrim learned many lessons in the house of the Interpreter. He saw a fire burning against the wall, and one standing by it to cast water on it to quench it, but yet the fire burned fiercer than ever. The Interpreter told him the meaning: "This fire is the work of grace that is wrought in the heart. He that casts water upon it to extinguish and put it out is the devil; but in that thou seest the fire notwithstanding burn higher and hotter, thou shalt see the reason of that." So he took Christian to the other side of the wall, and there was Christ continually pouring in the oil of His grace.

So it was with our Greatheart. Though the devil had

succeeded in quenching his zeal for a short while, the Lord's oil was poured on the nearby quenched flame, in response to his wife's prayers, so that he came forth from the trial a flame of fire that for the next sixty years became brighter and more intense every day. But we will let him continue his own story.

Wigglesworth Tells of Early Ministry

God gave me a great zeal in soul winning. Every day I sought to bring someone to Christ. I was willing to wait an hour any day to have an interview with anyone about his soul's salvation. At one place I waited an hour and a half, asking God to direct me to the one of His choice. The road was filled with people but I kept saying to the Lord, "I want the right man." After awhile I was somewhat impatient in my spirit and I said, "Lord, I don't have much time to waste." But God did not call it wasted time. After an hour and a half, a man came along with a horse and cart, and the Lord spoke to me just as He spoke to Philip when He told him to join himself to the chariot of the Ethiopian. I got up in the cart beside the man and was soon talking with him about his need of salvation. He growled, "Why don't you go about your own business? Why should you pick me out and talk to me?"

I wondered whether I had made a mistake. I looked up to the Lord and said, "Is this the right man, Lord?" He said to me, "Yes, this is the right man." And so I continued to talk to him and plead with him to yield his life to Christ. By and by I saw that he was shedding tears, and I knew that God had softened his heart and the seed of the Word was entering. After I was sure a true work of grace had been wrought, I jumped down from his cart, and he went on his way.

Three weeks later my mother said to me, "Smith, have you been talking to someone about salvation?" "I am always doing that, Mother." "Well, I visited a man last night. He was dying; he has been in bed for three weeks. I asked whether he would like someone to come and pray with him. He said, 'The last time I was out, a young man got into my cart and spoke to me. I was very rough with him but he was very persistent. Anyhow, God convicted me of my sins, and saved me.' " My mother continued, "That was the last time that man was out. He passed away in the night. He described the young man who talked with him and I could tell from his description that you were the one."

As I walked along, I would be always looking for someone to whom I could talk about the Lord. One time I went with a brother on a bicycle tour. Every day for ten days we had, on an average, three good cases of salvation. My experience in business life led me to a great many people whom I would not have contacted had I been a professional preacher. My whole business life was spent in communion with God. I sought to be His witness everywhere I went.

A man came to reside in Bradford and asked a business man: "Can you introduce me to a good plumber?" The business man replied, "Yes, I can, if you can stand his religion as well. He never goes out on a job but what he is preaching all the while he is doing his plumbing work." "Well," this man said, "I'll risk it." He told me afterwards that he was pleased that he had me as a plumber because of my talks to him about the Lord.

I was very successful in my plumbing work, but I was very poor in collecting the debts on my books. But every Saturday I had to pay my men. One day I was in need of money. I have always believed it was God's plan for me to be in need, because in the needy hour God opened the door to me and that strengthened my faith. At that particular time I went to the Lord and prayed, "Lord, I have not time to go out and seek money. Please tell me where I can get some." He said, "Go to Bishop." I had heard that he was a very bad payer and that everyone had to take him to the courts in order to get his money. But because the Lord had told me to go, I knew He could deal with him, so I went in faith.

As I went into the lodge gate, I met Mrs. Bishop coming out with another lady. I had been somewhat in hopes that I might see her and that she would pay me. So I said to myself, "There's only one hope and that is to see Bishop." But I hesitated for a moment because I knew that he paid nobody. Should I go? Well, I knew God had spoken to me, and so I went to the back door. The servant answered and I asked, "Is Mr. Bishop in?" "No, and he will not be home for three weeks." "I cannot understand that," I said. "Why don't you understand? You seem disturbed." "Yes, I am very disturbed. I have to have money to pay my men tomorrow, and as I have been praying the Lord directed me to come here; it is quite disturbing to know that Mr. Bishop is away and will not be back for three weeks." The servant asked, "How much is it that he owes you?" I said to her, "Just about twenty pounds ($100)." She said, "Come in." She went upstairs, brought the money down, and settled the account. I said to her, "Do you do this kind of thing often?" She answered, "No." Well, I knew the night previous the Lord had told me to go to that house at nine o'clock. She told me that at that very time the mistress had given her her wages and that she felt impressed to pay this account out of her wages. I said, "What makes you do it?" She answered, "I dare not let you go away without it. That is all I can say." God showed me how he could make a human impossibility possible. Incidents like that helped in the creation of a living faith in my heart.

One morning the children were all gathered around the breakfast table and my wife said, "Harold and Ernest are very sick this morning. Before we have breakfast we will pray for them." Immediately the power of God fell upon my wife and me, and as we laid our hands on these children they were both instantly healed. As we saw the miraculous healing wrought before our eyes, we were both filled with intense joy. The Lord was always so good in proving Himself our family Physician.

That day I went out to work at a house where a great many servants were employed, and I took an apprentice boy to work with me. I could see that the lady of the house was very restless. She came into the room where I was working, looked at me, and then walked out. Soon she came back and said, "Can't you send your apprentice to your shop for something?" I replied, "I was just going to send him to the shop because I am short one piece of pipe." As soon as the boy was out of the door she said, "Tell me, oh, please tell me, what is the cause of your face showing such a wonderful expression of joy?" I replied, "Well, this morning two of my children came to the breakfast table very sick. My wife and I prayed for them and God instantly healed them. I was filled with joy as I saw what He had wrought, and that joy is with me now." She said, "Please tell me how to get this joy. My house is full of trouble. My husband left me this morning after a big disturbance. Please tell me how I can get this peace and rest and joy that you have." I said to her, "The Lord has saved my wife and me, and we know what it is to have the power of God in our home, and for Him to meet all our needs and to fill us with His peace and joy." She said, "Oh, please, can you help me?" I said, "I can help you now."

She seemed afraid of the servants' coming in, so she locked the door and kept her hand on the key, as if she was afraid she might be disturbed any moment; and while she had her hand on the key, the Lord saved her. She was filled with the joy of the assurance that all her sins were washed away. She said, "Oh, how can I keep this?" I asked, "Do you have an 'at home' day when the ladies come to visit you?" She answered, "I have one next Thursday." I said to her, "Tell all the ladies how the Lord has saved you and ask if you can pray with them."

That was the ministry the Lord gave me all through the years that I was in the plumbing business. I had the joy of leading so many men and women, and so many servant girls, to Christ as I worked at my trade and witnessed for my Christ. The Lord had a purpose in keeping me tied up financially. In some respects I had a flourishing business but I was always short of ready money.

I can remember one day I went to prayer as usual and asked the Lord, "Where shall I go for money this weekend?" He said to me: "Go and see the architect and ask him for a certificate." I was working on a job under a certain architect, and so in obedience to the word of the Lord I went to see him. As soon as I got to the office he said, "What do you want?" I explained I needed a certificate. "On what job?" he asked. "The job you gave me to fix the furnaces in Osletgate." "Why," he said, "you have only just got to work." I replied, "That makes no difference, the work is done." The work was on a row of new houses. He said, "You couldn't have finished the work; I only gave it to you a week ago." I said, "When you gave it to me, you did so because you knew I would do it quickly." He asked, "How could you do it?" "I brought all my men from other work and got down to business." He doubted my word. He picked up his hat and said, "I will go and see." We went together and when he saw the work he was well satisfied. He said, "This is wonderful; it is just what we wanted." And so he wrote out a certificate for the money.

It was one thing to get the certificate and another thing to get the money. I started to the office of the mill master to whom the property belonged, and as I went I noticed on a shop window a scripture text, "Trust in the Lord at all times." I went forward, believing that since I had my trust in the Lord, everything would be all right. When I got to the office of the mill I handed the cashier the certificate. It was Saturday morning and he shouted louder than I could shout, "You'll get no money here! You'll get no money here! You'll get no money here! We never pay out money except on certain days in the month; and I tell you, you'll get no money here!"

He shouted so loudly that I thought there was something wrong with his mind. Behind him the door opened. The master appeared at the door and demanded, "Whatever is wrong?" I said, "I don't know, sir. I have given this man a certificate for payment and I don't know why he is shouting so." I gathered that the Lord made the clerk shout so as to bring the master down from another building. The mill master read the certificate and said to the cashier, "Pay this man his money. And if I hear of anything like this again, I'll fire you."

I came out of the office with the money and went down the street praising the Lord. When I came to the shop where I had seen that scripture text I went in and said, "How much do you want for that text?" I was told a shilling (25 cents), so I bought it and it was a great blessing to me to remind me continually to "trust in the Lord at all times."

Being in business for myself, I was able to devote much of my time to the sick and needy. I used to go to Leeds every week to a place where divine healing was taught. But I was very critical in my spirit and would judge people so harshly. I did not know why so many people who taught divine healing wore glasses. I questioned, "Why do you wear glasses if you believe in divine healing?" This stumbled me somewhat. Later I had to wear glasses to read my Bible, and I was often criticized for this. However, I was very full of compassion towards the sick and needy folks, and being able to pay the expenses of the needy ones, I used to collect a number of them and take them to Leeds every Tuesday to the service. One day I had nine with me. The leaders of the Leeds Healing Home looked through the window and said, "Here is Wigglesworth coming again and bringing a lot more. If he only knew, he could get these people healed at Bradford just as easily as to get them healed in Leeds."

These leaders knew that I had a compassion for the

sick and needy, and one day they said to me: "We want to go to the Keswick convention and we have been thinking whom we should leave to do the work. We can only think of you." I said, "I couldn't conduct a healing service." They said, "We have no one else. We trust you to take care of the work while we are away." A flash came into my mind: "Well, any number of people can talk. All I have to do is to take charge." The following week when I got there the place was full of people. Of course, the first thing I did was to look for someone who would do the speaking; but all whom I asked said, "No, you have been chosen and you must do it." And so I had to begin. I do not remember what I said but I do know that when I had finished speaking fifteen people came out for healing. One of these was a man from Scotland who hobbled on a pair of crutches. I prayed for him and he was instantly healed. There was no one so surprised as I was. He was jumping all over the place without his crutches. This encouraged the others to believe God for their healing and all the people were healed. I am sure it was not my faith, but it was God in His compassion coming to help me in that hour of need.

After this the Lord opened the door of faith for me more and more. I announced that I would have a divine healing meeting in Bradford on a certain evening. I can remember that there were twelve people who came that night and all of those twelve were miraculously healed. One had a tongue badly bitten in the center through a fall. This one was perfectly healed. Another was a woman with an ulcer on her ankle joint and a large sore that was constantly discharging. She was healed and there was only a scar the next day. The others were healed the same way.

One day a man asked me, "Does divine healing embrace seasickness?" I answered, "Yes. It is a spirit of fear that causes your seasickness, and I command that spirit to go out of you in Jesus' name." He was never seasick again though he had to travel much.

One day a man came to the house. He was a very devoted brother. I said to him, "Mr. Clark, you seem downcast today. What's up?" He answered, "I left my wife dying. Two doctors have been with her right through the night and they say she cannot live long." I said to him, "Why don't you believe God for your wife?" He answered, "Brother Wigglesworth, I cannot believe for her."

He went out of the house brokenhearted. I went to see a fellow named Howe who was opening a small mission in Bradford. I thought he was the right man to go with me, to assist me. When I said, "Will you go with me?" he answered, "No, indeed I won't. Please do not ask me again. But I believe if you will go, God will heal." I realized now that the Lord put those words in his mouth to encourage me.

Well, I knew a man named Nichols who, if he got the opportunity to pray, would pray all around the world three times and then come back. So I went to him and said, "Will you come with me to pray for Sister Clark?" He answered, "Yes, I will be very glad." We had a mile and a half to walk to that house. I told him when he began to pray not to stop until he was finished. When we got to the house we saw that Mrs. Clark was nearly gone. I said to the one I had brought with me, "You see the dangerous condition of Sister Clark. Now don't waste time but begin to pray." Seeing he had an opportunity, he began. I had never suffered so much as I did when he was praying, and I cried to the Lord, "Stop him! Please, Lord, stop this man's praying." Why? Because he prayed for the dear husband who was going to be bereaved and for the children who were going to be motherless. He piled it on so thick that I had to cry out, "Stop him, Lord; I cannot stand this." And thank God, he stopped.

Though I knew that neither Clark nor Nichols believed in divine healing, I had concealed a small bottle in my hip pocket that would hold about half a pint of oil. I put a long cork in it so that I could open the bottle easily. I took the bottle out of my pocket and held it behind me, and said: "Now you pray, Mr. Clark." Brother Clark, being encouraged by Brother Nichols' prayer, prayed also that he might be sustained in his great bereavement. I could not stand it at all, and cried, "Lord, stop him." I was so earnest and so broken that they could hear me outside the house. Thank God, he stopped.

As soon as he stopped, I pulled the cork out of the bottle, and went over to the dying woman who was laid out on the bed. I was a novice at this time and did not know any better, so I poured all the contents of that bottle of oil over Mrs. Clark's body in the name of Jesus!

I was standing beside her at the top of the bed and looking towards the foot, when suddenly the Lord Jesus appeared. I had my eyes open gazing at Him. There He was at the foot of the bed. He gave me one of those gentle smiles. I see Him just now as I tell this story to you. I have never lost that vision, the vision of that beautiful soft smile. After a few moments He vanished but something happened that day that changed my whole life. Mrs. Clark was raised up and filled with life, and lived to bring up a number of children; she outlived her husband many years.

Everybody has to have testings. If you believe in divine healing, you will surely be tested on the faith line. God cannot bring anyone into blessing and into full cooperation with Him except through testings and trials.

My wife and I saw that we could not go just half-measures with God. If we believed in divine healing we would have to be wholeheartedly in it; so we pledged ourselves to God and then to each other. This consecration to trust God seemed to bring a new order in our lives. We looked into each other's faces and said, "From henceforth no medicine, no doctors, no drugs of any kind shall come into our house." It is very easy when in health and strength to make pledges and utter vows, but it is being faithful when the time of testing comes that counts. Little did we know that shortly we were going to have such a test.

We were both very zealous for the Lord and spent a good deal of time in open-air meetings. One Sunday a violent pain gripped me and brought me down to earth. Two men supported me and brought me home. The same thing had happened before, but the pain had not been so severe in previous times. We prayed all night. The next morning I said to my wife, "It seems to me that this is my home-call. We have been praying all night, and nothing has happened; I am worse. It does not seem as though anything can be done. You know our arrangement is that when we know we have received a home-call, only then to save each other the embarrassment of having an inquest and the condemnation of outsiders, would we call a physician. To protect yourself, you should now call a physician. I leave it with you to do what you think should be done."

Poor thing, she was in a sad plight, with all the little children around her and there seemed no hope whatever. She broke down, and left me and went to see a physician—not for him to help me, for she did not think he could help me, but believing that the end had come.

When the doctor came he examined me, shook his head, and said, "There is no hope whatever. He has had appendicitis for the past six months and the organs are in such shape that he is beyond hope." He turned to my wife and said, "I have a few calls to make, Mrs. Wigglesworth. I will come and see you again later. The only hope is for him to have an immediate operation, but I am somewhat afraid your husband is too weak for that."

When he got out of the room, an elderly lady and a young man came in. She was a great woman to pray, and she believed that everything that was not health was of the devil.

While she prayed, the young man knelt on the bed with both knees, laid his hands on me and cried out, "Come out, devil, in the name of Jesus."

To my surprise the devil came out and I felt as well as I had ever been in my life. I was absolutely free from pain. As soon as they had prayed for me they went downstairs, and I got up, believing that no one had a right to remain in bed when healed. When I got downstairs, my wife cried, "Oh!" I said, "I am healed." She said, "I hope it is true." I inquired, "Any work in?" "Yes, there is a woman who is in a great hurry to get some plumbing done; if we could not take care of it, she would have to go somewhere else." She gave me the address and I went out to do this work. While I was working, the doctor returned. He put his silk hat on the table, went upstairs, got as far as the landing, when my wife shouted, "Doctor! Doctor! Doctor! Oh, Doctor, he's out. He has gone out to work." The doctor answered, "They will bring him back a corpse, as sure as you live." Well, the "corpse" has been going up and down the world preaching the gospel these many years since that time!

I have laid hands on people with appendicitis in almost every part of the world and never knew of a case not instantly healed.

IV

"ENDUED FROM ON HIGH"

~~~~~~~~~~~~~~~~~~~~~~~~~~~~~~~~~~~~~~

WE CONTINUE the story in our Greatheart's own words.

Wigglesworth Tells of Receiving Baptism

My wife was a great preacher, and although I had no ability to preach, she made up her mind to train me for the ministry. So she would continually make an announcement that I would be the speaker the next Sunday. She said she was sure I could preach if I only tried. When she announced me to speak, this would give me a week of labor and a good deal of sweating. I used to go into the pulpit on Sunday with great boldness, give out my text, say a few words, and then say to the congregation, "If any of you can preach, you can have a chance now, for I am finished."

She would have me try again, but it always ended the same way. She was the preacher and I encouraged her to do it all. But I found out that when you have a burden for lost souls, and the vision of their need is ever before you, the Lord, as you look to Him, will give you expression to your heart's compassion and make a preacher out of you. We held open-air services for twenty years in one part of the city of Bradford. It was as I ministered in the open air week by week that the Lord began to give me more liberty.

My wife and I always believed in scriptural holiness but I was conscious of much carnality in myself. A really holy man once came to preach for us and he spoke of what it meant to be entirely sanctified. He called it a very definite work of grace subsequent to the new birth. As I waited on the Lord for ten days in prayer, handing my body over to Him as a living sacrifice according to Romans 12:1, 2, God surely did something for me, for from that time I began to have real liberty in preaching. We counted that as the baptism in the Spirit. And so at our mission on Bowland Street we stood for both healing and holiness.

We never believed it was right for us to do all the preaching. And so we gave two or three of our young men and women a chance every week. These young workers developed and the result was that many of them became wonderful preachers.

We thought that we had got all that was coming to us on spiritual lines, but one day we heard that people were being baptized in the Spirit and were speaking in other tongues, and that the gifts of the Spirit were being manifested. I confess that I was much moved by this news.

One day I saw a man coming to the house and noticed that he had very great difficulty in getting up the steps to our front door. But he managed to pull himself up some way or other by the railing, and when he had taken a seat he said: "If my people knew that I was coming to your house, they never would have let me come. You have a worse name than any man I ever heard of." I said, "If that is your opnion of me you had better clear out of my house, for I do not want anyone here that does not believe in me."

"Oh," he said, "I believe in you. Please do not put me out. If you knew my terrible condition, you would not send me away. Put your hand on my leg, will you?"

I did, and found it was like a board, not like a leg. I said, "It feels strange. What's the trouble?"

"It is a cancer. All the leg, from top to bottom, is cancerous. Oh, you will not send me away, will you?"

I replied, "I will not send you away. I will go and see what God says about this." As I waited before the Lord these words came to me: "Go, tell that man to fast seven days and seven nights, and his flesh shall become like a little child's."

I told him what the Lord had given me for him, and he said, "I believe all that God has said to you, and I will go home and do all that God has told me to do."

Four days later I was looking through the window and here was this same man; but instead of having to take hold of the railing and pull himself up like a sick man, he jumped up those steps and came running around the house like a boy, crying out, "I am perfectly healed!" I asked, "What are you going to do now?" He answered, "I am going back to fast a further three days and three nights, but I thought I would let you know what God has already wrought."

The next time he came to our house he saw my daughter Alice and heard her say that she was going to Angola in Africa. "I would like to have a share in this," he told her as he pulled out a handful of gold coins, saying: "That's my gift towards your going to Africa." Then he turned to me and remarked, "Have you heard the latest? They are receiving the Holy Spirit at Sunderland and speaking in other tongues. I have decided to go up to Sunderland to see this thing for myself. Would you like to come with me?" I declared that I would be delighted to go. He said, "All right, you come along with me and all expenses will be paid out of my purse." He was so happy at having been healed, and he surely was glorifying God for the miracle that had been wrought in his life.

I wrote ahead to Sunderland to two people who had been saved in the work in Bradford and who had gone to live in that town. The report had come to them that what was happening was a very dangerous error and that speaking in other tongues was from an evil power. In order to save me from this terrible error they arranged for a very wonderful woman to be on hand to warn me. And so the first things I heard were false reports. When they had said all they had to say, I suggested, "Let us pray." The Lord gave me real liberty in prayer and after I had prayed they said, "Don't take any notice of what we have said. Obey your own leadings."

It was a Saturday night when I went to the meeting, which was held in the vestry of the parish church at Monkwearmouth, Sunderland. What I could not understand was this: I had just come from Bradford, where the Spirit of God was working mightily. Many had been prostrated, slain by the power of God the night before I left for Sunderland. It seemed to me that there was not the power in this meeting that we had in our own assembly in Bradford. I was disappointed.

I went to meeting after meeting, and I am afraid I discouraged them all, for I would get up and speak: "I have come from Bradford and I want this experience of speaking in tongues like they had on the day of Pentecost. But I do not understand why our meetings are on fire, but yours do not seem to be so." They told me to be quiet, that I was disturbing the meeting. But I was very hungry for God, and He knew my hunger even though nobody seemed to understand me.

I can remember a man giving his testimony that after waiting on the Lord for three weeks, the Lord had baptized him in the Holy Spirit and caused him to speak in other tongues. I cried out, "Let's hear these tongues. That's what I came for. Let's hear it!" They answered, "When you are baptized you will speak in tongues."

According to my own opinion I had been baptized in the Spirit. Thinking back to my ten days of waiting on God and the blessing I had received as a result, I had called that the baptism in the Spirit. So I said to them, "I remember when I was baptized, my tongue was loosed. My testimony was different." But they answered, "No, that is not it."

But I was seeking with all my heart after God. On a Sunday morning I went to a Salvation Army prayer meeting at seven o'clock. Three times in that prayer meeting I was smitten to the floor by the mighty power of God. Somewhat ashamed of my position, lest I should be misunderstood, I tried to control myself by getting up again and kneeling and praying. At the close of the service the captain said to me, "Where are you from, Brother?" I answered, "I am from Bradford. I came to Sunderland to receive these tongues that people are getting here." "Oh," he said, "that's the devil they are getting up there." But anyhow, he invited me to preach for him that afternoon, and we had a very wonderful time. But they were all persuading me not to go near the Pentecostal people and not to seek the speaking in other tongues.

That night in the vestry of that parish church we waited on the Lord until about twelve o'clock. I was there again on Monday morning. I am afraid I disturbed the meeting again that morning. After the meeting a missionary from India followed me out and said, "You are spoiling all our meetings. You claim to be baptized with the Holy Spirit and yet you are creating a disturbance at every meeting that you attend." I sought to vindicate myself, and our conversation terminated very unpleasantly.

Pastor Boddy, who was vicar of the Episcopal Church where those first Pentecostal meetings were held, gave out a notice that there would be a waiting meeting all night on Tuesday. It was a very precious time and the presence of the Lord was very wonderful, but I did not hear anyone speak in tongues. At 2:30 in the morning Brother Boddy said, "We had better close the meeting." I was disappointed, for I would have liked to stay there all night. I found I had changed my clothes and left the key to my hotel room in the clothes I had taken off, so the missionary brother from India said to me, "You'll have to come and sleep with me." But I did not go to bed; we spent the night in prayer and received great blessing.

For four days I wanted nothing but God. But after that, I felt I should leave for my home, and I went to the Episcopal vicarage to say good-bye. I said to Mrs. Boddy, the vicar's wife: "I am going away, but I have not received the tongues yet." She answered, "It is not tongues you need, but the Baptism." "I have received the Baptism, Sister," I protested, "but I would like to have you lay hands on me before I leave." She laid her hands on me and then had to go out of the room. The fire fell. It was a wonderful time as I was there with God alone. He bathed me in power. I was conscious of the cleansing of the precious Blood, and I cried out: "Clean! Clean! Clean!" I was filled with the joy of the consciousness of the cleansing. I was given a vision in which I saw the Lord Jesus Christ. I beheld the empty cross, and I saw Him exalted at the right hand of God the Father. I could speak no longer in English but I began to praise Him in other tongues as the Spirit of God gave me utterance. I knew then, although I might have received anointings previously, that now, at last, I had received the real baptism in the Holy Spirit as they received on the day of Pentecost.

V

AFTER RECEIVING THE BAPTISM

~~~~~~

Wigglesworth Continues His Story

AT THE time I received the baptism in the Spirit, a meeting was going on in the large vestry of the All Saints Church, and I went straight to it. The vicar of the church, Pastor Boddy, had charge and he was speaking. I knew that as yet he had not received the baptism in the Holy Spirit, and I interrupted him by saying, "Oh, please let me speak, Mr. Boddy; I have just received the baptism in the Holy Ghost."

The place was full of people. I can't remember what I said, but I know I made all those people extremely dissatisfied and discontented with their position. They said, "We have been rebuking this man because he was so intensely hungry, but he has come in for a few days and has received the Baptism and some of us have been waiting here for months and have not yet received." A great hunger came upon them all. From that day God began to pour out His Spirit until in a very short while fifty had received the Baptism.

The first thing I did was to telegraph to my home saying, "I have received the baptism in the Holy Ghost and have spoken in tongues." On the train to my home town, the devil began questioning, "Are you going to take this to Bradford?" As regards my feelings at the moment, I had nothing to take, but the just do not live by feelings but by faith. So I shouted out on the railroad coach to everybody's amazement, "Yes, I'm taking it!" A great joy filled me as I made this declaration, but somehow I knew from that moment it would be a great fight all the time.

When I arrived home one of my sons said to me, "Father, have you been speaking in tongues?" I replied, "Yes, George." "Then let's hear you," he said. But I could say nothing, for although I had received the baptism in the Holy Ghost, I had not received the distinct gift of tongues. That did not come until nine months later. My son did not understand that the speaking with tongues which accompanies the receiving of the baptism in the Spirit is not the "gift of tongues" spoken of in I Corinthians 12. The former is given as evidence that the Spirit has come in Pentecostal fulness; but there may not be any further utterance in tongues unless there is a special anointing of the Spirit. The "gift of tongues," however, is such that the receiver may use it for prayer or praise at any time.

My wife said to me, "So you've been speaking with tongues, have you?" I replied, "Yes." "Well," she said, "I want you to understand that I am as much baptized as you are and I don't speak in tongues." I saw that the contest was beginning right at home. "I have been preaching for twenty years," she continued, "and you have sat beside me on the platform, but on Sunday you will preach yourself, and I'll see what there is in it."

She kept her word. On Sunday she took a seat at the back of the building. We had always sat together on the platform until that day. So the contest had begun right in the church.

There were three steps up to the platform, and as I

went up those three steps the Lord gave me the passage in Isaiah 61:1-3, "The Spirit of the Lord God is upon me; because the Lord hath anointed me to preach good tidings unto the meek; he hath sent me to bind up the brokenhearted, to proclaim liberty to the captives, and the opening of the prison to them that are bound." I was no preacher, but hearing the voice of my Lord speaking those words to me, I began. I cannot now remember what I said, but my wife was terribly disturbed. The bench on which she sat would seat nine people and she moved about on it until she had sat on every part of it. Then she said in a voice that all around her could hear, "That's not my Smith, Lord, that's not my Smith!"

I was giving out the last hymn when the secretary of the mission stood up and said, "I want what our leader has received." The strange thing was that when he was about to sit down he missed his seat and went right down on the floor. Then my oldest son arose and said he wanted what his father had, and he, too, took his seat right down on the floor. In a short while there were eleven people right on the floor of that mission. The strangest thing was that they were all laughing in the Spirit and laughing at one another. The Lord had really turned again the captivity of Zion and the mouth of His children was being filled with laughter according to the word of the Lord in Psalm 126:1, 2.

That was the beginning of a great outpouring of the Spirit where hundreds received the baptism in the Holy Ghost and everyone of them spoke in tongues as the Spirit of God gave utterance.

God knew that I should have to go all over the world and proclaim this glorious truth, that all could receive the baptism in the Holy Ghost in exactly the same way as they received on the Day of Pentecost with the speaking in other tongues as the Spirit of God gives utterance.

The first call that I received after I had been baptized in the Holy Spirit was from a man who had a factory in Lancashire, and who employed more than 1000 people.

He wrote to say he had heard I had received the Holy Spirit as at the beginning, and he would like to meet a man who had had this experience. His letter said, "If you will come, I'll close down the factory each afternoon and give you five meetings between 1:00 p.m. and 11:00 p.m." I wrote back, "I'm like a great big barrel that feels like bursting if it doesn't have a vent, so I'm coming to you for the meetings."

Up to that time I had had no preaching abilities, but then I felt that I had a prophetic utterance which was flowing like a river by the power of the Holy Spirit. So I went to Lancashire; and that manufacturer closed down his factory, and from 1:00 p.m. to 11:00 p.m., with short intervals, I was preaching. Surely Christ fulfilled His promise, "He that believeth on me, as the scripture hath said, out of his belly shall flow rivers of living water." Quite a large number in that factory were gloriously saved.

Soon after this my dear wife received the baptism in the Spirit, and then we went forth together in response to the many calls that came from different parts of the country. Wherever we went the Lord baptized people with the Holy Spirit.

We went together to a small place in Shropshire where we held a meeting in a Primitive Methodist Chapel. As my wife preached, the fire fell and people were baptized in the Holy Spirit all over that chapel. There was a good deal of opposition and plenty of persecution. It was a small country village and everyone round about seemed to be greatly moved. They all knew about that revival in that church.

The next morning after the "fire had fallen," I went walking around the village and entered a grocery shop. A deep conviction fell on three people who were in that shop and before I left that grocery store all three were saved. After I came out I went up the road a little and saw two women in a field who were carrying buckets. I shouted out to them, "Are you saved?" Here again a tremendous conviction seized them. They dropped their

pails and began to pray; and right in that field the Lord
saved those two women.

Wherever I went conviction seemed to be upon people. I went into a stone quarry where a whole lot of men
were employed, and I preached to them as they were
dressing the big stones, and again conviction fell and
many were saved. As I was returning from this quarry, I
passed a large saloon. Just as I was nearing it two men
drove by in a two-wheel vehicle, and I never have seen
men with such evil faces. They looked the very picture
of the devil. I did not know who they were but as they
came near they cursed me and tried to slash their whip
at me. It seemed like a whiff from the pit. They shouted
so loudly that the landlord and landlady at the hotel and
five people came out of that saloon and dashed at me
like mad dogs, cursing and swearing, though I had not
spoken a word to them. But I did not fear their assault.
I cried out instantly, "In the name of Jesus, in the
power of the blood of Jesus, I drive you back into your
den." They rushed back into the hotel and I went in and
preached Jesus to them.

There were many people healed and baptized at that
time and the glory of the Lord constantly fell. Twenty
years later I visited that same village and the people re-
counted the story of that wonderful visitation from
God. Many people from different parts of the country
would come to our mission and on almost every occasion they would express the wish that I would visit their
place and do something for them.

I had many telegrams to go to a place near Grantham
to a young man who was very dangerously ill. After I
arrived at Grantham I had nine miles to go by bicycle.
When I came to that farm house that afternoon a
woman at the door asked, "Are you Wigglesworth?" I
replied, "Yes." She said, "I am sorry to say that you are
too late. My son is beyond anything being done for him
now." I answered, "God has never sent me anywhere
too late."

I asked if I could see the young man. He lay in his

bed with his face toward the wall and whispered that if he was turned over he would die, for his heart was so weak. "Well," I said, "I'll pray for the Lord to strengthen you." In most of my work in those early days I used to pray much and fast. I knew that this case was beyond all human hopes, and so I lay awake most of the night praying. I got up very early the next morning and went out to an adjoining field to pray, for I was very much burdened about this case. There in that field God gave me a revelation that this had to be something new in my life.

I went into the house and asked them to put their son's clothes to air because the Lord would raise him up. In that part of England the climate is very damp, so I knew it would be necessary for them to put his clothes before a fire before he could wear them. But they did not believe and so did not do anything about his clothes.

That was Sunday morning and I knew that there was a service at the Primitive Methodist Chapel. I went to the service and was invited to take charge. Through the word of the Lord, faith was planted in the hearts of all those people, and then something happened. They all knew that young man by name, and they all said, "Matthew will be raised up!" That led me to see that faith could be created in others just as it had been created in me, and I went back to that house and said, "Have you put his clothes to air?" I think they were a little ashamed that they had done nothing, so they got out his clothes and put them before the fire. Then I went into the room and told the young man the vision I had, and said that something would happen different from anything that I had experienced before. I said, "When I place my hands on you the glory of the Lord will fill the place till I shall not be able to stand. I shall be helpless on the floor." I went out and got his clothes, and said to one of the household, "All I want you to do is put his stockings on him."

Why I had asked them to put his stockings on is a

mystery. His legs were like those of a skeleton and I saw his helplessness, and knew that a miracle would have to be performed. After this member of the household had put the stockings on the young man I said, "Now you can leave the room."

They shut the door. I think it is a very important thing to have the door shut when you have a case like this to deal with, for then you know that you are just shut in with God. I prayed for the vision to be made good, and instantly, the moment I touched the young man, the power of God filled the room and was so powerful that I fell to the floor. My nose and my mouth were touching the floor and I lay there in the glory for a quarter of an hour. All that while Matthew in the bed was shouting, "Lord, this is for Thy glory! This is for Thy glory!" The bed simply shook, as did everything in the room, by the power of God. Matthew's strength, his life, and his heart (which was considered the weakest thing about him) were all renewed. I was still on the floor in the glory when he arose from his bed and began to dress. After he was dressed he began to walk up and down the room shouting, "I'm raised up for Thy glory! I'm raised up for Thy glory!" Opening the door he shouted, "Dad, God has healed me. I'm healed!" The same glory filled the kitchen; the father and mother fell down; and the daughter who had been brought from the asylum and whose mind was still affected was made perfectly whole that day.

That whole village was moved and a revival began that day. I went into that village unnoticed and unknown, but when I left all the village turned out and shouted, "Please come back, please come back, and stop with us longer next time."

I made the nine miles back to Grantham and paid a visit to one of our converts who had moved to this city. The moment I got to the door she said, "My brother is going to take you to a man who has cancer on the bladder." I went with her brother to the house of a sick man and before I reached the house I could hear a voice crying out, "Oh, dear! Oh, dear! Oh, dear!" It was so loud I could hear it at least fifty yards before I got to the home. When I got into his room he was still shouting, "Oh, dear! Oh, dear!"

Instantly God revealed to me that neither this man nor his wife were saved, so I said to the man, "This great affliction is as much mental trouble as cancer. Are you saved?" "Oh," he cried, "If I were saved I could die comfortably. If I were saved I would not mind this cancer or anything." I pointed out the way of salvation, and God saved the man and his wife. That man had such a revelation of salvation that joy overflowed, and I could hear him shouting "Hallelujah" for fifty yards after I left that home. The transformation was beyond all description. He had no more trouble with that cancer. I hurried to the station and caught my train back to Bradford.

I soon saw that my business would have to give place to the ministry that God was giving me. I had supported my family with my plumbing business; but I was called out of town so often, and people could not wait—they had to seek help from other sources. Each time I returned to Bradford I had less business.

There came a period of very severe frost. I went around to my various customers and helped them to cover up their water pipes so they could get water during the frosty weather, but I knew that when the thaw came I should be wanted at many places to repair broken pipes.

I was invited to a convention at Preston in Lancashire. During those convention days the frost broke and telegrams began coming in asking me to return immediately to Bradford to do repair work. At that time the leader of the convention said to me, "You've helped us much and have been a very great blessing, and we would very much like you to stay until the end of the convention; but if you feel you want to go home we will relieve you." I went home but I found out that most of my customers who had had broken pipes had been compelled to seek other plumbers. There was only one woman, a widow, who had not been able to get a plumber. I went to her house and found that it was flooded with water and that one of the ceilings was down. I was so sorry for her that I repaired her pipes and her roof. She was grateful, for she had waited many days for help. When she said, "Tell me how much I owe you now," I answered, "I won't receive any pay from you. I'll make this an offering to the Lord as my last plumbing job."

A friend once remarked: "All the people who say they live by faith seem to have their heels worn out, and their clothes are old and green." I believed that God would abundantly provide if I served him faithfully. I promised Him at that time that I would obey Him implicitly, but I laid down the condition that my shoe heels must never be a disgrace, and I must never have to wear trousers with the knees out. I said to the Lord, "If either of these things take place, I'll go back to plumbing." He has never failed to supply all my needs. He increased my vision and faith and gave me calls all over England. I was a pioneer with the Pentecostal message to a great many assemblies throughout Great Britain. Soon calls began to pour in from other countries also.

I had a lot of money on my books that I was not able to collect without court action, but I preferred losing it to going to law. All the debts that I owed at that time were met by a young friend whose heart the Lord opened to make me a gift of some fifty pounds (approximately $250.00).

My wife and I continued our ministry at Bowland Street, Bradford, even though I had to be frequently absent because I was ministering elsewhere. I believed in house-to-house visitation, and I prayed in every house I entered. Everywhere I went souls were saved and people were healed.

I was not ashamed of the gospel, so I purchased the largest flag pole that could be obtained and placed it outside the mission. I had a flag waving on that pole three yards long and one and one-half yards wide. One side of the flag was red and the other side was blue with white letters. On one side, I had the scripture, "I am the Lord that healeth thee." On the other side, "Christ died for our sins." That flag had great effect on the people who saw it when passing by.

God moved me on to a place of increasing faith, causing me to see that the Word of God was written to show us how to *act* on the principles of faith. I saw that Christ had said, "When thou makest a feast, call the poor, the maimed, the lame, the blind: and thou shalt be blessed; for they cannot recompense thee: for thou shalt be recompensed at the resurrection of the just." So I engaged two people to go out and find all the needy, the sick, and the afflicted and I gave them tickets inviting them to a banquet and entertainment at the Bowland Street mission.

After the two people had gone round the neighborhood they gathered together a great company of needy people. That sight was beyond all description. There were the blind and the halt and withered. All around the mission there were wheelchairs and people on crutches and the blind were being led. This was the best day in my life up to that point. I wept and wept and wept. One reason I wept was because of the great need; I was weeping also for joy at the opportunity, and with expectation of seeing things that I had never seen before. And so it was.

The first thing we did was to supply everybody with a first-class meal, and there was plenty to spare of the very best we could provide. After they were filled we gave them entertainment, not in a worldly sense, but the whole program was surely very entertaining. The first man on the program was one who had been wheeled up and down in a chair for a very long time, who told how he had been healed by the power of God. The next one on the program was a woman who had been healed of an issue of blood. She told how she was healed by prayer and by the anointing of oil the day before she was to go on the operating table.

Then we had a man who had been going about trailing his foot and his arm because he had had a paralytic stroke. He told how he was healed after the doctors had given him up.

For an hour and a half we kept those poor helpless people deeply moved and weeping by the stories they heard of how Jesus could heal the sick. I said to them, "Now we have been entertaining you today, but we are going to have another meeting next Saturday and you people who are today bound and who have come in wheel chairs, and some of you folks who have come like the woman in the gospels, who had spent her all on doctors and was no better, are going to entertain us on Saturday night by the stories of the freedom that you have received today by the name of Jesus." So we prayed for those people and God mightily met us. We surely had a great time the following Saturday night as one after another told of how God had healed them of their different infirmities.

I shall never forget that day. I cried out, "Who wants to be healed?" Of course, everyone wanted to be. I remember one particular case. I had gone to fetch a woman in her wheelchair. The wheel was broken, but I managed to fix it up. I helped her from her home, but that wheelchair gave way in the road. I said to her, "Well, you will never want it again anyhow." I fixed it again and ultimately we arrived at the mission. God so marvelously healed her that she walked home, and I am a witness to the fact that she went up all the steps into her house and into her bedroom praising the Lord as she went.

There was one young man who had been having epileptic fits for eighteen years who was instantly healed. He had never gone out without having someone to accompany him. His mother brought him to that meeting, and God so wonderfully undertook for him that within two weeks he was working in a factory and bringing home wages.

Another case was that of a young man who was all doubled up like the woman in the Bible. Jesus called it the spirit of infirmity, indicating that she was bound by an evil spirit. That day that young man was loosed and set free just as the woman was loosed in the synogogue. Christ in His healing ministry said He was working the works of God, and He said that if we believed, we also could do the works of God. He had cast out the spirit of infirmity; so I cast out the spirit of infirmity in the name of Jesus, and immediately the young man was made straight, and everyone was blessing the Lord for the miracle they saw.

Another remarkable case was that of a boy who, from his head to his feet, was encased in thin iron. The building was very crowded but the father lifted up the boy in the iron case and passed him over to the man who was sitting in the seat in front of him. He was then passed on to the next seat and others passed him on until ultimately he was placed before me on the platform. I anointed him with oil and laid hands on him in the name of Jesus, and immediately he cried out, "Papa, Papa, Papa. It's going all over me! It's going all over me! It's going all over me!" And he was loosened that day and made absolutely free.

Can you wonder that faith was quickened in the hearts of many as they saw these miracles wrought? A week after, these people were going around as witnesses telling what Christ had done for them.

VI

THE MINISTRY OF HEALING

~~~~~~~~~~~~~~~~~~~~~~~~~~~~~~~~~~~~~

WE HAVE often heard Smith Wigglesworth say that it did not matter where he went in the Scripture for a text, he nearly always ended up preaching that the Lord not only forgives all sin but heals every disease.

His constant message was *"Christ."* He would say of Him: "There was never One who came into the world with such loving compassion and who entered into all the needs of the people as did Jesus. And He declares to us, 'Verily, verily, I say unto you, he that believeth on Me, the works that I do shall he do also; and greater works than these shall he do, because I go unto My Father.' God wants us all to have an audacity of faith that dares to believe for all that is set forth in the Word." But we will let him continue his own story.

Wigglesworth Continues His Story

One day I was in Sweden. While I was walking along I saw a man fall into a doorway. There was immediately a throng around him, and they said he was dead. I immediately used the power and authority of the name of Jesus, and instantly that man was delivered. He had been troubled that way for many years. The Lord told me to make him a public example, so I invited him to come to the meeting, and he came and told of his deliverance. He mentioned the most awful things that the devil had been telling him, and then he told us that the devil had gone right out of him.

While I was in Ceylon I was sent to a certain place to pray for a woman, who was surely in a terrible condition with cancer, and nearly dead. The house was full of people, and I preached Christ to them. I said, "I know this woman will be healed, but I want you to know the power of my Lord. I want you to know Him who can save you from sin and can deliver you from all the power of the devil." I prayed for the woman, and her deliverance was so marvelous and it had such an effect upon the people in that home that they went to the newspapers and had the story published. The woman herself came to the meeting and told how the Lord had completely healed her. Christ told us, "These signs shall follow them that *believe.*" What is it to *believe?* It is to have such confidence in what the Lord said that we take Him at His word, simply because He said it.

I remember one day that I was asked to visit a woman who was dying. When I got into the room where the woman was, I saw that there was no hope as far as human aid was concerned; she was suffering from a tumor and it had sapped her life away. As I looked at her, I knew that there was no possibility of help except the Lord would work a miracle. Thank God I knew He was able. I said to the woman, "I know you are very weak, but if you wish to be healed and cannot lift your arm, or raise it at all, it might be possible that you could raise your finger." Her hand lay upon the bed, but she lifted her finger just a little.

I said to my friend, "We will pray with her and anoint her." After we had anointed her, her chin dropped. My friend said, "She is dead." He was scared. I have never seen a man so frightened in my life. "What shall I do?" he asked. You may think that what I did was absurd, but I reached over into the bed and pulled her out. I carried her across the room, stood her against the wall and held her up, as she was absolutely dead. I looked into her face and said, "In the name of Jesus I rebuke this death." From the crown of her head to the soles of her feet her whole body began to tremble. "In the name of Jesus, I command you to walk," I said. I repeated, "In the name of Jesus, in the name of Jesus, walk!" and she walked.

My friend went out and told the people that he had seen a woman raised from the dead. The woman's doctor heard of it and went to see her. He said, "I have heard from Mr. Fisher, the elder, that you have been brought back to life, and I want you to tell me if that is so." When she affirmed it he asked, "Dare you give your testimony at a certain hall if I take you in my car?" "I will go anywhere to give it," was her willing reply. She came to the hall looking very white, but there was a lovely brightness on her face. She was dressed in white, and I thought how beautiful she looked.

This is what she said: "For many months I have been going down to death, but now I want to live for my children. I came to the place where it seemed there was no hope. I remember that a man came to pray with me and said, 'If you cannot speak, or cannot lift up your hands, if you want to live, move one of your fingers.' I remember moving my finger, but from that moment I knew nothing else until I was in the Glory. I feel I must try to tell you what the Glory was like. I saw countless numbers of people; and oh, the joy and the singing! It was lovely, but the face of Jesus lit up everything. Just when I was having a beautiful time the Lord suddenly pointed to me without speaking, and I knew I had to go. The next moment I heard a man say, 'Walk, walk in the name of Jesus!' If the doctor is here, I should like to hear what he has to say."

The doctor arose and tried to speak, but he could not at first. His lips quivered and his eyes looked like a fountain of water. At last he said that for months he had been praying. He felt that there was no more hope, and he had told them at the house that the woman would not live much longer. In fact, it was only a matter of days. He acknowledged that a miracle had been wrought through the name of Jesus. That doctor wrote to a friend of his and said, "If you ever get a chance to hear Wigglesworth, you must certainly do so; hundreds of people have been healed in this place."

I received many telegrams and letters asking me to go to pray for a certain woman in London. They did not give me full details. I only knew that the woman was in great distress. When I arrived at the home the dear father and mother of the needy one took me, one by one hand and the other by the other hand, and broke down and wept. Then they led me up into a balcony. They pointed to a door that was open a little and they both left me. I went into that door and I have never seen such a sight as that in my life. I saw a beautiful young woman, but she had four big men holding her down to the floor, and her clothing was torn as a result of the struggle.

When I entered the room and looked into her eyes they rolled, but she could not speak. She was exactly like that man who saw Jesus and ran to him when he came out of the tombs, and as soon as he got to Jesus the demon powers spoke. The demon powers that were inhabiting this young girl spoke and said: "I know you." You can't cast us out; we are many."

"Yes," I said, "I know that you are many, but my Lord Jesus will cast you all out." It was a wonderful moment. It was a moment when He alone could cope with the situation. The power of Satan was so great upon this beautiful girl that in one moment she whirled and broke away from those four strong men. The Spirit of the Lord was wonderfully upon me, and I went right up to her and looked into her face. I saw the evil powers there; her very eyes flashed with demon power. "Though you are many," I cried, "I command you to leave at this moment, in the name of Jesus." She instantly began vomiting. During the next hour she vomited out thirty-seven evil spirits and she named every one of them as they came out. That day she was made perfectly whole. The next morning at ten o'clock I sat at the table with her at a communion service.

*   *   *   *   *

During a visit to Los Angeles in 1948, I was told the following incident by the one who entertained Wigglesworth at the time he was holding a tent meeting in that city. He had just begun to preach one night in the tent when there was great commotion in one of the front seats. A lady had fainted. A number gathered around her. Wigglesworth cried out, "I rebuke you, you evil devil, for disturbing this meeting." Immediately, all over the tent, people were criticizing him for his harshness.

But the sequel to this incident justifies his action. A few days later the husband of the woman who had fainted came to the house to see Mr. Wigglesworth. "My wife has been sick for years," he explained, "and I have had to wait on her. Every morning I would have to carry her breakfast to her bedroom on a tray. But everything is different since the night you rebuked that evil power in her. The next morning she said to me, 'You won't have to bring my breakfast to me this morning. I am perfectly healed, and I'm going to get up and prepare the breakfast myself.' And she has done this every morning since. Doubtless she has been oppressed by a spirit of infirmity, but since you rebuked it the other night when she fainted, the thing has gone and now she is perfectly free."

During the latter years of Smith Wigglesworth, he was accompanied by his son-in-law, James Salter, and by his daughter, Alice. The latter undertook most of his correspondence and the former greatly helped to minister faith to the different audiences as he told of the many remarkable miracles and signs that have followed the preaching of the Word in the Belgian Congo in Africa. Mr. and Mrs. Salter tell of hundreds of miracles which they saw following the prayer of faith of our Greatheart.

Like his Master, he was a man of authority. He was called to pray in Kansas City for a demon-possessed woman. When he reached the home the demon power in the woman was most violent in its curses. He commanded the evil spirits in the name of Jesus to depart. He then prepared to leave the home. All the way that he walked to the door the woman followed him, and from her mouth there poured out a tremendous volume of curses. He did not say, "I guess I did not pray the prayer of faith; I had better go back and pray again." To him such a course would have been failure. He turned and spoke to the demon power in that woman with authority saying, "I told you to leave." That was enough. The woman was completely delivered and her pastor stated later that she had no recurrence of demon possession.

All the following cases of healing recorded in this chapter have been told us by Mr. James Salter. Wigglesworth would often startle us in a meeting by saying, "Just to let you see that the Lord is in our midst and His power is present to heal and to bless, we are going to have an exhibition, a demonstration. In the Acts of the Apostles we read of 'All that Jesus began both *to do* and *to teach.*' His doing preceded His teaching. Every sermon that Christ preached was prefaced by a model miracle. We are going to follow His example. The first person in this large audience that stands up, whatever his or her sickness, I'll pray for that one and God will deliver him or her."

James Salter Continues the Story

How often our hearts have quaked as we have heard him make that bold announcement, for there would be cancers, consumptives, people in wheelchairs, others lying on folding beds, twisted, pitiful cases of all kinds of diseases. Secretly we have hoped that one of the simple cases would stand, and not one of the far-gone cancer cases or deformed cripples.

On one occasion we shook in our seats as, in answer to his challenge, a poor, twisted, deformed man, having two sticks for support, struggled to his feet.

When Brother Wigglesworth saw him, he did not turn a hair. In his characteristic manner he asked, "Now, you; what's up with you?" After he had taken stock of the situation, he said, "All right, we will pray for you." He had the whole assembly join with him in prayer, and then, addressing the man, he said, "Now, put down your sticks and walk to me." The man fumbled for a time; then he let his sticks fall to the ground and began to shuffle along. "Walk, walk!" Brother Wigglesworth called, and the man stepped out. "Now run," he commanded, and the man did so to the amazement and great joy of all who were present, and to our unbounded relief!

In Sweden his preaching on divine healing and water baptism so stirred up the doctors and some ministers of religion that they combined in presenting a petition to their parliament. This resulted in Brother Wigglesworth being forbidden to touch the people or lay hands on any of them in public for their healing. One day he was preaching in a park when it was estimated that a crowd of at least 20,000 people had gathered to hear him. A number of government representatives were present to insure that he carried out the law—and he was equal to the situation. He asked all who were sick to stand if they could; and failing that, to indicate in some way their need and he would pray for them. He said, "Now each one lay hands on himself and I'm going to pray

that the Lord will heal you." The sick people laid their
hands on their own afflicted parts, and he prayed a simple prayer of faith. Hundreds were blessed and healed
as a result. In this way he kept within the law.

During his latter days he used this simple method on
scores of occasions when he had a very large audience
and he knew it would take hours to pray for everyone
who needed help. Thus it was that in a park in Stockholm, Sweden, was born what he later referred to as his
"wholesale healing" method. Actually this was forced
upon him by the action of the Swedish government. It is
quite safe to say that hundreds of people were healed by
this method and that such healings were permanent.
(See chapter nine for Mr. Wigglesworth's own description of this first experience in wholesale healing.)

In one large city where we had two meetings a day
for a month, this method was used every day because of
the huge crowds who sought his ministry. One man had
sat in front of the platform in an endeavor to get some
idea of what the preacher said. He had been deaf for
forty years. During one of these wholesale healing dem-
onstrations he suddenly began to swing his head about
in a fantastic way and then ran out of the tabernacle.
He returned to the evening service to testify. He said
that he had been stone deaf for forty years, but that
during the morning meeting, while the preacher prayed,
something seemed to snap in his head and a noise like
the firing of a big gun filled his ears. That was why he
ran out of the building, up to the top of the road, and
from there he could hear the preacher's voice quite
plainly. During the rest of the services, he was so
pleased that he could hear that he sat on the back seat
and in the farthest corner from the speaker so that all
would know that he now could hear quite well.

In the same meeting was a war veteran whose spine
had been damaged by a bullet wound. During a wholesale demonstration he too was perfectly healed. Two or
three people were healed of cancers at the same time. A
little boy was lifted up on a table. One of his legs had

been two inches shorter than the other. His father raised him to tell the audience what had taken place. The boy testified, "When the preacher told the folks to move their arms or legs or whatever was diseased, I pushed out my short leg and it became just as long as the other one." The result of this miracle was seen by about 1500 people.

During the same campaign one woman stood up and said, "I am a great sufferer. I have been in the hands of the doctors for a long time, and at present I have a floating kidney, gallstones, and chronic appendicitis." Along with many others she arose at the time of the "wholesale healing demonstration," and when prayer was made she was perfectly healed. There were hundreds of people blessed, healed, and delivered in those meetings by that method, and although those meetings were twenty years ago the results are permanent. Only today (November 19, 1947) here in Los Angeles, California, a lady stood up and testified that she was healed in those services.

In a large city in Arizona, a center to which thousands of tubercular people came to live in the desert surroundings to take the cure, we had a series of meetings. The news spread very rapidly among those folks and some traveled considerable distances to be present in the services. There were rich and poor—all classes and in all stages of lung trouble. Here also he used his wholesale healing method among the people. One lovely young lady, far advanced with the disease, rose as he made his challenge. "Stand out in the aisle," he called to her, and she did so, her bosom heaving with excitement and her cheeks flushing. Through the great effort she was gasping for breath. "Now," he said, "I am going to pray for you and then you will run around this building." He prayed and then he shouted, "Run, woman, run." She said, "But I cannot run. I can scarcely stand." "Don't talk back to me," he called; "do as I have said." She was reluctant to move, and so he jumped down from the platform and urged her to run. He helped her a little, and she clung to him until she gathered speed; finally she galloped around that big auditorium without any effort. When seen some considerable time later, she was quite well.

There was another woman in the same meeting that he told to "run." When she showed her reluctance and would not start, he pushed her. She clung to him, and together they ran around the building a few times. Her legs had been locked by sciatica and her feet were so crippled that she could scarcely walk. God completely delivered her, and every day after that she walked to the meetings instead of using the street car because she was delighted to have the full use of her limbs again.

He called his dealing with individuals "retail healing." A lady stood in line one day in Leeds, England, waiting for a bus. A nurse in uniform was next to her and they engaged in conversation. They discovered that they were both Christians and then the talk turned to the subject of sickness. The woman told the nurse that she had a son with a diseased thumb and she contemplated taking him to the hospital. "Don't do that," said the nurse; "they may take it off. I'll give you the address of someone who will pray for him and the Lord will heal his thumb." By this time the bus had arrived, and although it was not going in the way the nurse wished to travel, she boarded it with the lady so that they might continue the conversation. On the bus the woman said to her, "I, too, am sick. I have a cancer on the breast." Taking a small book from her bag, the nurse wrote on it the name and address of Smith Wigglesworth. "Write to him and you will get a reply." Having finished her work for God, the nurse alighted at a convenient stop.

The sick woman wrote to Brother Wigglesworth, so we went to visit her and found the cancer in an advanced stage. Prayer was made for her, and then we left to make the twenty-five mile journey home. God completely delivered the woman, making her well and strong in her body. Feeling extremely well, she undertook to decorate her house. While emptying a cupboard she found an old Bible, and on opening it her eyes fell on a passage she had underlined with red ink. It read, *"Thine health shall spring forth speedily."* She had marked that passage twelve years previously; then had forgotten it and had not claimed the promise of God's word. Her faith was strengthened by her experience and by the Word that had been fulfilled so literally to her. Some years have elapsed since this incident, but she has had no further trouble with the cancer.

In Acts 19:11, 12 we read, "And God wrought special miracles by the hands of Paul: so that from his body were brought unto the sick handkerchiefs or aprons, and the diseases departed from them, and the evil spirits went out of them." Special miracles in hundreds of cases were wrought through handkerchiefs that Brother Wigglesworth sent to sick people, and hundreds of letters were received telling of the miracles that were wrought. Volumes could be written containing nothing but answers to such cases. Every kind of sickness and disease has been placed in pillow cases, in sleeping suits, etc., and drunkards have lost appetites for strong drink; smokers have left off tobacco; wayward sons and daughters have been brought back to Christ; separated couples have been re-united. They have been used for every conceivable kind of need, trouble, and sickness.

There is one especially interesting case of a lady who sent for and received a handkerchief. She said she was in a dying condition with cancer. When the handkerchief arrived, she placed it on her pillow, intending to apply it in the presence of her husband and family. While lying there she began to feel the presence of God from the nearby cloth until a healing in her body took place. Today there is no sign of cancer. Smith Wigglesworth always made it clear that behind all the methods or means used was Jehovah the healer, and that Jesus Christ is the same yesterday, today, and forever.

He was always unpredictable. He sometimes did things that were extraordinary, but later on we found that he had really been led by the Holy Spirit. On one occasion as he was ministering before a very large audience, he seemed needlessly severe in his dealing with a lady and she fell to the floor. "Lift her up," he said, and again she fell. This time some of the people nearby remonstrated with him, but he answered that he knew his business, that he was dealing with a devil and not with a woman. Again she was lifted to her feet, and as she stood a huge cancer fell from her to the floor. That was the answer.

Frequently his methods were misunderstood and his motives were misinterpreted. Yet he persevered lovingly with a single eye toward God and a holy sincerity toward the people. He was not moved by criticism. He would say, "I am not moved by what I see or hear; I am moved by what I believe."

Doors were opened to him everywhere, but there were many adversaries. At the height of one of his mightiest revivals, at the time when thousands of people were being healed, a woman who was apparently crippled was wheeled into the church. Prayer was requested for her and so Smith Wigglesworth prayed for her in his usual manner. About a week later a letter arrived from her lawyer making financial claims for damages to this woman. The case was not a genuine one, yet it was accompanied by a doctor's certificate and the claim was pressed. The whole claim was a fake, but the money that was demanded was paid in order to avoid legal proceedings.

"He was moved with compassion," was Smith Wigglesworth's daily experience. Tears would run copiously down his cheeks as he ministered to the afflicted. How tender he could be in dealing with children and aged folks! How he would valiantly storm heaven with his praying for the pain-racked and suffering ones.

Race distinction was a thing unknown to him. Black, red, yellow, all sought his ministry and all were blessed by his prayers and his gifts. He ignored social distinctions in his ministry, and he could be very severe on anyone who sought private claims on his attention on such grounds.

In one city he was working hard for a month with three meetings each day. God was at work among the people. Cancers were cured, legs strengthened, the deaf were being healed, all manner of healings were being wrought, and best of all souls were being saved. One day the chief pastor, who had built and paid for the hall where the meetings were being held, and who also had two assistant pastors, said, "There is a lady in this city who is very ill. I feel that if she would be healed the effect on the people would be very great. Would you visit her, Brother Wigglesworth?"

He replied that he was very busy with three meetings each day, with praying for the sick and assisting those who were seeking to be baptized in the Holy Spirit, and that this did not leave him very much free time. However the pastor persisted and pressed the matter from day to day, emphasizing the social standing of the lady and her husband in the city; and also the effects that such a healing was bound to have on all who knew them.

"Well," said Brother Wigglesworth, "how can we fit in such a visit?" It was finally decided that the call should be made on our way to the evening meeting. Because of the status of the lady and her family all three pastors accompanied Smith Wigglesworth, my wife, and me to the house, which was located in the best part of the city.

We drew up at the door, rang the bell, and were ushered into a palatial room. From there we moved into a very large bedroom. There like an eastern monarch on a throne sat the gorgeously robed lady in a rainbow-colored pile of lovely embroidered cushions.

Smith Wigglesworth stood and stared at such a sight. Then he said, "Well! You certainly look comfortable!" "I beg your pardon," she snapped. "I said, 'You look very comfortable!' " She let loose in a storm of abuse which left her exhausted. "Oh!" he said, "I can see that you are not ready for me yet. Good evening." And so saying he walked out of the house and entered the waiting automobile.

My wife and I followed him out and ventured to suggest that he had been a bit harsh with the lady. "I know my business," he said. The pastors remained in the bedroom for some while in an endeavor to placate the lady. When they came out they pleaded with him to go back and pray with her, but he was adamant, saying: "No, she is not ready for me; let us go to the meeting."

We were all much disturbed in our spirits over the affair. But if he felt anything, he certainly did not show it, for he went through the service with a mighty unction of God upon his preaching and upon his praying for the sick.

The next morning we had the service at the usual time. The Spirit of the Lord was graciously with us and at the close of the address an invitation was given to all who wished to "come nearer to God." He said, "If you move forward only a foot, you will be blessed; if you move forward a yard, you will get more. If you come up to the platform we will pray for you, and God will meet your needs with His supply." All the audience moved, but a stately lady led them. In her desire to be first to get to the front, she fell prostrate. It was the lady whom we had left in the bed the previous evening. After we had left her she had deeply repented. God had healed her, and now at the morning service she publicly consecrated her life to God. She was a broken woman, profuse in her apologies. Again we had been wrong in our judgments, and God had vindicated Smith Wigglesworth's action.

On November 28, 1947, I was in Bethel Temple, Los Angeles, and was told the following three incidents. A man stated; "I was born in Norway and heard Brother Wigglesworth there about twenty-two years ago. I was dying with tuberculosis. One lung had already collapsed; but after he prayed for me, God healed me and I put on twenty-six pounds in weight in a very short time. Then we moved to America and lived in Chicago.

My wife was very ill with lung trouble and spit blood continually for three years. I took her to one of Brother Wigglesworth's meetings in Chicago. She was prayed for and delivered from her sickness. We had had no children up to this time, but after my wife's healing the doctor found that she was pregnant. He remarked, 'It is a great tragedy. It certainly will mean the death of mother or child.' Both survived the ordeal. Two more children also were born, and the children and the mother are well and strong."

Another family—husband, wife, two grown-up daughters and a son—presented themselves to us at the close of the service. They had traveled more than 120 miles to be present at the meeting. They had written to Brother Wigglesworth for a prayed-over handkerchief. The father was suffering from acute appendicitis and the son had a large growth on his neck. When they applied the cloth, the father's pains all ceased and he was healed of the appendicitis. The lump on the boy's neck burst, the swelling disappeared, and he has had no further trouble with that over a period of years. The man said, "We were not able to let your father-in-law know about this, but we have traveled all this distance to tell you. We thank God for his ministry."

Another person came to us in the same meeting and said: "I was with Brother Wigglesworth in England for a whole day and we had meals together in his home in Bradford. In the afternoon he took us to a nearby park where we sat and talked for awhile. During that short period he led two men to the Lord, and he prayed for two others for the healing of their bodies. He seemed to be so busy that my friend and I decided to take a short walk. When we returned we found him kneeling by the side of another man pointing him to the Lord Jesus. He prayed and preached all the time we were with him and appeared to live for God for the help of other people."

Smith Wigglesworth would give no place to the devil, and to outsiders at times he seemed to be extremely rough and uncouth. The following incident sets forth his attitude toward the devil. One day when he was waiting for a bus, a little dog attached itself to a lady standing near him. Evidently she had hurried out of the house thinking she had left the dog behind her. Somehow it had gotten out and followed her, to her annoyance. She bent down and patted it on the head and said, "Now, you must run home, dear; I cannot take you with me." The dog's response was to wag his tail until all his body shook, but he made no move towards home. "You really must go home now, my little pet," she said sweetly. By that time the bus was in sight and she was desperate. Stamping her foot she said severely, "Go home at once!" The little dog was scared by such an attitude; he put his tail between his legs and scampered off as fast as his legs could take him. "That's how you have to treat the devil!" Wigglesworth said loudly enough for all who were waiting for the bus to hear.

James H. Taylor of West Roxbury, Mass., wrote of a meeting of Wigglesworth's in Washington, D.C.: "I think it will help our testimony to state that we had seats in the second row from the healing corner, so that what happened during the healing hour was almost within hand reach. Just before the meeting began, we had noticed that a young girl with crutches was coming in. She was assisted by a man and woman. Her legs absolutely dangled, with the feet hanging vertically from them. From her waist she seemed to be limp and powerless. Room was made for her in the front row. When the invitation to be saved was given, she attempted to go forward aided by her assistants. Brother Wigglesworth, on seeing her start, said, 'You stay right where you are. You are going to be a different girl when you leave this place.' When the rest had been dealt with Brother Wigglesworth turned to the girl and, having been told her trouble, said to the people, 'This girl has no muscles in her legs; she has never walked before.' He laid his hands on her head and prayed and cried, 'In the name of Jesus Christ, walk!' Looking at her, he said, 'You are afraid, aren't you?' 'Yes,' she replied. 'There is no need to be. You are healed!' he shouted. 'Walk! walk!' And praise God she did—like a baby just learning! Twice she walked, in that characteristic way the length of the platform! Glory to God! When we left the room, her crutches were lying on the seat, and on reaching the sidewalk we saw her *standing, as others do,* talking with two girl friends. Glory to God in the highest and on earth—*healing to those who believe.* Amen.

"The woman who assisted her forward was her mother, and the man was her uncle; he wept like a child during her healing. He testified in the evening meeting that she walked up the stairs at her home without assistance, repeated the fact that she had never before walked, and stated that her mother, who went forward for healing for a growth on her breast, when asked about it said, 'It's gone!'

"Wonderful things happened at the evening meeting also. One brother testified to the healing of a cancer of two years' standing. A poor sick man whom the doctors had given up, whose legs were useless, except for slow motion, was healed and *ran* twice around the hall! When asked how many had been healed during the week's services, at least two hundred arose. Well, what shall I say—but praise God?"

VII

IN LABORS MORE ABUNDANT

~~~~~~

I LABORED more abundantly than they all," Paul declared, but he was quick to add, "yet not I, but the grace of God which was with me."

Our Greatheart's life, like the apostle's, was "in labors more abundant," but he was quick to acknowledge that it was all of grace and by faith that his labors were accomplished. To him the attitude of faith was not one of strain, of effort, nor of crying and moaning night and day, but just one of laying hold of God's gracious provision, and trusting and resting. He knew God could not fail in His promises. He believed the record that God "hath given unto us all things that pertain unto life and godliness," and so he laid hold in living faith of the exceeding great and precious promises, and his expectation of an exhibition of God's power was constantly fulfilled.

Once more we will let our Greatheart resume his own story.

Wigglesworth Tells of Foreign Ministry

God has blessed me in so many ways. I have seen sight restored to persons born blind. I have seen three persons come to life after being dead. All these things that I have passed through only make me to know that Christ's promises concerning the greater works are true, and we must give Him all the glory for them.

It was my privilege to labor in India and in Ceylon, and to see God mightily moving there. Probably the high point of the revival was at Colombo. How God blessed!

I was preaching under the anointing of the Spirit and a crowd gathered. They packed the place to suffocation. But the power of God was wonderful. After preaching, and that through an interpreter in a temperature of about 120 degrees, we prayed for about 500 sick people each night.

In that great heat, women would bring their babies. We would sometimes have fifty or more in the meeting, and because the atmosphere was so oppressive they would be crying. I used to say, "Before I preach I will minister to the babies." It was very wonderful, as soon as hands were laid on these babies, to notice the silence, the quietness, the peace, and the order of those meetings! The power of God was there. One man in the midst of this great crowd, who had been blind for a long time, was healed. His eyes were opened instantly. We saw many similar miracles take place.

I cannot understand how God can give to any of His children glory and virtue, but it nevertheless is true that He does. There were thousands of people that could not get into the meeting, but as I passed out through the great crowd the people that could not get inside reached out and touched me, and they were healed. I marvel at the grace of God that it could take place. There is something about believing in God, that makes God willing to pass over a million people just to anoint you. I believe God will always turn out to meet you on a special line if you dare to believe Him.

I was in one place for only four days, and they were disappointed that I could not stay longer. I said to them, "Can you have a meeting early in the morning, at eight o'clock?" They said they would. I said, "Tell all the mothers who want their babies to be healed, to come; and all the people over seventy." It would have done you good to see 400 mothers coming in at eight o'clock with their babies, and then to see about 150 old people with their white hair, coming to be healed. In those days there were thousands out to hear the Word of God. I believe there were about 3,000 persons crying for mercy at once. It was a great sight.

I arrived one day in Norway at about nine a.m., and said to my friend who was interpreting for me, "Nobody knows that I am here, so please take me down to the fjords. I would like to relax, because I am so tired." We had a few hours in the sunshine and rested, and then came back. When I returned I found that the street all around the building where I was to speak was filled with every kind of vehicle with wheels on, and these were filled with needy sick. The brother who was to interpret for me ran to the top of the step of the building and said, "What shall we do? The house is full of people." I took off my coat, got into every wheeled vehicle there and prayed for the people. There was great shouting in the street as God healed them; and then I went into the house and God healed them there also.

But that was not all. We sat down to eat, and while we were eating the telephone rang, and the message came: "What shall we do? The Town Hall is full and there are thousands outside. The police cannot do anything with the crowd." I said, "We will come down as soon as possible." Two policemen got hold of me and pushed me through the crowd. When I got inside that Town Hall, I never saw anything so packed! I have seen sardines packed—yet these people couldn't have fallen down if they had wanted to! The Spirit of the Lord was upon me. I began to preach. I have forgotten my subject but I knew I was eaten up with the zeal of the Lord.

I cried to God for a message that would be different, that something might happen in that meeting different from anything else. As I was preaching, I heard the voice of God speaking and saying, "If you will ask Me, I will give you every soul." I went on preaching and God repeated: "If you will ask Me, I will give you every soul." I knew it was the voice of God, yet I was slow to accept. Then the voice of the Lord came again: "If you will believe and ask Me, I will give you every soul." I looked up to Him and said, "All right, Lord, please do it. I ask You, please give me every soul." The breath of the Holy Spirit swept over the whole place and I have never seen anything like it. All over, cries for mercy! I believe that God gave me every soul. That is my conception of Pentecost. Pentecost is believing that after the Holy Ghost comes upon you, you have the power. Do not be afraid to believe. Believe that God makes you a partaker of the divine nature through His great and precious promises. His own eternal power working in you will bring forth a divine order that can never be surpassed by anything in the world.

* * * * *

Smith Wigglesworth preferred throughout his whole life to be unattached to any religious body. His heart of love went out for all the saints. We have been with him in different towns where he would search out the Salvation Army to be with them at their prayer meeting at seven a.m. and then he would frequently go to the Episcopal Church to their Holy Communion service at eight a.m. On three different occasions he held meetings for Episcopal ministers. If they wanted it, he would put on the surplice and cassock, which they considered a necessity for ministry. One Episcopal minister arranged a tent meeting for him in London—such an innovation was frowned upon by his bishop; but this minister's son had been healed through Mr. Wigglesworth's ministry, and he wanted others to be benefited by the same. Incidentally, one time when King George V was sick, this Episcopal minister's wife sent a handkerchief to him that our Greatheart had prayed over, and received a letter of thanks for sending the same.

The Assemblies of God in Great Britian would usually invite him to their annual conference. They wanted all the young men to receive the benefit of his inspirational ministry. He, however, would not attend any of the business sessions, saying, "You carry on, and I will pray for you." And so he would turn aside and give himself to prayer.

Having no denominational affiliation, he had no human backing in his travels, and so he frequently arrived in places with no other recommendation or support than the reputation he had achieved through his ministry. This was especially so in many countries in Europe which he visited after the first world war. He arrived in Switzerland a complete stranger, but God was with him in mighty power. Towns were moved for God and he was constantly invited to return to that land. He had many blessed meetings there.

When he arrived in New Zealand he had just one man to meet him; but thousands were won for God there, being saved, healed, and filled with the Spirit through his few months of ministry. It was stated that it was the greatest spiritual visitation on the North Island known for more than a century. As a result of his ministry, some 2,000 sat down to "break bread" in one of his Sunday morning meetings in Wellington.

There was no body of people to meet him when he stepped from his ship in Colombo, Ceylon. His arrival was almost unnoticed, but he had not been there many days before the whole district was throbbing with the power of God. Crowds thronged to touch him, and scores who stood in his shadow were healed and blessed.

Somehow, his fame usually spread ahead of him, and

on one occasion when his ship put in at one of the Pacific Islands, he was kept busy preaching and praying for the sick until the boat departed. He was tireless in his zeal to help the needy.

When he arrived in Palestine the first time, he was a complete stranger, but it was not long before he was preaching the gospel and praying for the sick. On the mount of Olives he had some blessed services and quite a number were filled with the Holy Spirit as on the day of Pentecost. He aroused the district so tremendously that the departure of the Jerusalem-Haifa train was delayed so that he could finish his sermon to the people who had gathered to hear him. All the way to Egypt he sat in earnest discussion with influential non-Christian men, who on arrival at Alexandria took him with them to lunch so that they could continue the conversation about the things of God. About this visit to the Holy Land, he laughingly remarked that he thought he was the first Gentile preacher who ever received an offering from the Jews there. God often used him in his journeys on trains and on steamers. He told us of an experience on a train.

"I remember once I was traveling to Cardiff in South Wales. I had been much in prayer on the journey. The carriage was full of people whom I knew to be unsaved, but as there was so much talking and joking I could not get in a word for my Master. As the train was nearing the station, I thought I would wash my hands so I should be ready to go straight to the meeting. I went along the corridor, and as I returned to the carriage, a man jumped up and said, 'Sir, you convince me of sin,' and fell on his knees there and then. Soon the whole carriage of people were crying out the same way. They said, 'Who are you? What are you? You convince us all of sin.' It was a great opportunity that God had given me, and you may be sure that I made the best of it. Many souls were born into the kingdom of God in that railway carriage."

On his way to Australia he wrote:

"I began quietly to work among the passengers and testify to the power of God, and I found this was very convincing. One was telling another about me, so I got an open door. A gentleman and a lady who were very rich occupied a first-class cabin, and their valet and his wife were traveling second-class. We had morning and evening services conducted by the Bishop of Bombay and they were very good. After a morning service the Bishop and I had a long talk together, and he was very interested in my work.

"After the evening service the valet and his wife were seeking me, as the lady was very sick. They had called the doctor, who had pronounced her very ill. The valet had told the lady about me and she desired an interview. She was really very sick and also filled with the principles of Christian Science, and finding these had failed her, she was in great fear. So I told her about the only principle I knew and that principle was Jesus; but she knew nothing about Him. I prayed with her, laid hands on her, rebuked the demon in the name of Jesus, and the fever left her at once. This morning she is seeking salvation through the Word of God. She is now on deck, full of life, and I had the pleasure of dealing with the valet and his wife about their salvation also."

Wigglesworth's son-in-law, James Salter, writes of him: "What a lonely figure he seemed to be on the deck of the giant liner with its thousand passengers when he was leaving for Australia the first time. As the ship left the dock, he lifted his voice repeatedly in a series of hallelujahs, with a clarity and volume I have never heard equalled. He startled his fellow-passengers and caused the captain on his bridge to remark, 'That man has lungs of steel!' It was on this ship that he was asked to take part in a concert. He asked to be the last item on the program. The pianist said she could not accompany him when he gave her a hymnbook; but that did not matter. He sang his solo, a hymn exalting Christ. That concert turned into a soul-saving prayer meeting, and the dance scheduled to follow the concert was abandoned."

On one occasion he made a promise to help a young man who was starting a work for God in a new and very difficult district. He was ministering on the Pacific Coast, and Mr. and Mrs. James Salter were there helping him. He heard that this young man, who was on the Atlantic Coast, was needing him. He did not mind paying out approximately five hundred dollars for railroad fare and Pullman accommodation to get to the Atlantic Coast to fulfill his promise to that young minister. When the first service commenced in the afternoon, there were just six people present (not counting his own party) in a large auditorium that would accommodate 5,000 people. It was not a very encouraging start, but before the campaign concluded the audiences were filling that huge place and that young man got his chance to start a new assembly.

His zeal sustained him in tropical heat, when he was surrounded by hordes of flies, which hovered around the children with pus-filled eyes, and in the stench of crowds of men and women suffering from nauseating tropical diseases. He could be equally zealous in icy Norway or Finland, preaching and praying for the sick, while one interpreter after another had to drop out owing to fatigue.

He was frequently told, "You cannot hold three meetings a day in this city; the people will not turn out, and even if they do, that is too much for any preacher." But he would hold his three meetings a day, and the people would turn out to hear him, and he would survive such an ordeal for a month at a time. Even in the biggest tent meetings and under the most trying conditions, he maintained his vigor week after week. He proved that the Lord's "yoke is easy, and His burden is light." He delighted to do God's will. His meat was to do the work he believed God had given him, and to fulfill his ministry. The joy of the Lord sustained him all through his life.

He put in more work on Sundays than on any other day. For a number of years he would be in the open-air preaching service until late on Saturday night. He would follow this up with a prayer meeting. But he would be up early on Sunday morning to put things in order at the church for the day's meetings. In the winter time he would attend to the heating of the building, do much of the dusting of the seats, praying over each one as he dusted it, arrange the table for the communion service, and lead the early morning prayer meeting. In the early days, his wife did most of the preaching as well as entertaining the many folk who constantly filled their home. The Sunday night service always found needy souls and bodies at the altar, and usually it was very late at night before the Wigglesworths got home. After that, the fellowship would continue in the house around a well-filled table until long past midnight.

Our Greatheart and his wife were model spiritual parents, not only bringing converts to birth, but nursing and feeding them on the Word of God, and laboring in prayer that each one might stand complete in all the will of God. Their practical Christianity as well as their precepts, their combination of holy life and godliness have been the incentive and mainspring to many a young life as he started on his work for God. Christian workers from all over the world praise God for the inspiration that these lives have given them.

Mr. Salter says: "Untiring and indefatigable all through his life, it was only a short time before he died that we noticed any change, and that he made any reference to his age. He arrived home from a convention where he had worked very hard—unusually hard, even for him. We noticed his tired look when we met him at the railway station. That evening in our prayer time he said, 'I cannot understand some of these young preachers these days. Fancy a man of my age preaching three times a day and praying for the sick at each service. Some of them will take the afternoon off and go to bed, leaving me to preach. When I was their age I would preach all the day, and then pray and tarry all night with those who were seeking to be filled with the Holy Spirit.' Thus he wrought with labor and travail night and day, and he labored till the going down of the sun."

VIII

MIRACLES IN AUSTRALIA AND NEW ZEALAND

~~~~~~

IT WAS in the early part of 1922 that Wigglesworth made his first visit to Australia.

We quote from a letter (which appeared in the English paper, *Confidence*) written by Miss Winnie Andrews of Victoria: "Our dear Brother Wigglesworth arrived in Melbourne last Thursday, and he had a meeting that night . . . and although he made it quite plain and clear to his hearers that he would rather see one sinner saved than ten thousand people healed of bodily ailments, he invited any who were in pain to come forward for prayer . . . Among those who came forward were several who later declared they had received remarkable and instantaneous healings. One little girl, six years of age, after prayer by the evangelist, was seen walking out of the front door of the building with her mother, who was delightedly exclaiming to all and sundry: 'Look at her! She has never walked in her life before!' A man who had not walked for over four years, owing to rheumathoid-arthritis, was instantly healed, and after triumphantly passing his stick and crutch up to the platform, gave an impromptu exhibition of the power that had come into his legs, by jumping and leaping and praising God.

"Since the first night there have been many other wonderful healings. Last night a dear woman who had been unable to walk for six and a half years was brought to be prayed for, and—glory to God!—she got out of her chair and walked. Her husband pushed her chair along while she walked behind.

"There have been many conversions—at one meeting alone, forty accepted Jesus as their Lord and Saviour. The revival showers are falling and God is working."

Some may ask the very reasonable question, "Do the healings last?" We have before us a sheaf of testimonies of healings that were prepared fifteen months after our Greatheart's visit to Australia. In it there are eighteen testimonies of remarkable healings in this first Australian campaign. We have also a copy of the *Australian Evangel* of February 1, 1927, in which there are thirteen testimonies of people who were healed in this campaign that was held five years before. We have also a copy of the *Australian Evangel* of March 1, 1927, which contains the story of one who was raised from a living death five years before. The testimony is so remarkable that we will let it speak for itself. It is written by Mrs. W. E. Brickhill (nee Kathleen Gay) of Victoria.

Woman Reports Remarkable Healing

"At the age of seventeen years, from a life of worldliness and sin, I received the Lord Jesus Christ as my own personal Saviour, being truly born again. It was a wonderful morn when I awakened with the consciousness that I had passed from death unto life, from the power of sin and Satan into the glorious liberty of the children of God.

"However, after sixteen months of unmarred service

for the Lord, an unfortunate accident occurred which caused serious injury to my abdomen, and brought on internal complications, necessitating consultation between four surgeons, who advised that an operation was imperative. The operation did not have the desired effect, and, to my sorrow, proved unsuccessful, laying the foundation for nearly fourteen years of continual suffering, the major portion of which time I was confined to bed.

"Later it was discovered that consumption, with all its cruel and devastating ravages, had gripped my entire being. This terrible disease wrought havoc with my constitution, causing sleeplessness for days and nights at a stretch. I got rest only when drugs were administered, and eventually my condition became such that drugs had no effect other than to cause a comatose state.

"All the symptoms of tuberculosis were evident, eating into my internal organs and having the effect of destroying my appetite entirely. The condition of my digestive organs was such that I refused almost all food, and invariably the little food partaken of was vomited immediately. Sometimes it was not possible to retain even a drink.

"Many leading specialists, surgeons, and physicians prescribed, without effect; in fact, many times they vouchsafed the opinion that my end was very near and that there was nothing more to be done.

"The deadly work of this disease was manifested to a very great extent upon my kidneys, which were perforated, and hemorrhage was very frequent. Outward evidences of the disease appeared in my left arm, thigh and hip, all of which presented the usual discharging sores connected with this malady. These parts of the limbs were so severely attacked that they presented an emaciated appearance, being repulsive to the sight, the bone being eaten into, a condition undoubtedly beyond all human aid. Having been reduced nearly to a skeleton, weighing only forty-two pounds, and being told by physicians that six weeks was the extent of my life, I was not fearful of my fate, as it seemed to me that death would relieve me of all my sufferings.

"While lying in this dying condition early in February, 1922, a ray of light entered my soul through word coming to me that an evangelist from England was holding meetings in our city of Melbourne and was preaching the gospel of Jesus Christ and His power to heal the sick. This evangelist was Smith Wigglesworth, and it was stated that he would pray for the sick. As the news was conveyed to me, I began to receive faith in God and expressed a desire that he should come and pray for me at my home; but learned that there were so many demands upon the evangelist's time, prayer for me at my home was impossible. The news caused the enemy to discourage me, but, praise the Lord, further faith being received, and being desperately anxious for victory, my parents were consulted. After much pleading to be allowed to be taken into one of the meetings, they reluctantly consented.

"Therefore, on February 16, as a very last resort, in my awful condition, I was assisted into one of the Sunday meetings. As the meeting progressed, my faith began to rise, and truly I realized the nearness of God. It was a hallowed time indeed. At length the evangelist was directed towards me, and on ascertaining that it was a consumptive case, he spoke sincerely to me and said: 'Sister, I believe the Lord will heal you; fear not, only believe.' My eyes saw no man save Jesus; I waited for His divine touch. After being anointed and prayed for, the power of God permeated my whole being and I was instantly healed. All the pain, weakness, and disease ceased. Hallelujah! My chains fell off. My soul was free, I arose, and went forth praising God, realizing a mighty work was done.

"Immediately after the Lord met me, my first desire was to hasten home and tell how great things had been accomplished in me. Even on my return journey I bore testimony of the fact by being able to walk unaided. On arrival at home I acquired a ravenous appetite for food, an unheard-of occurrence with me for years. Our household was filled with anxiety for my well-being as they watched me appease my hunger, fearing all the natural consequences from taking food would return; but to their amazement, I thoroughly enjoyed a hearty meal with satisfaction.

"After dinner, with assistance, the bandages were removed from the affected parts of my body. It was found that the Lord had replaced decayed bone and ulcerated flesh with new, beautifully healthy flesh and bone covered with white skin similar to that of a little child. All my senses became quickened, and that night I was able to enjoy a beautiful night's rest, the first natural sleep since the time I became sick.

"It is now five years since the Lord's hand so definitely rested upon me, and He has continuously overshadowed me with His presence, and filled me with His Spirit. The Lord provided work for me to do in His vineyard soon after He healed me as a Sister in the slum life of our city where, through His wonderful grace, many souls have been won for Him. Along with me in this work is my husband, whom the Lord gave me in a wonderful way three years ago.

"It is my sincere desire that my evidence of the power of God to heal will be used to help some soul in doubt to believe God and find that He is faithful to His Word that 'all things are possible to him that believeth' (Mark 9:23), and 'Jesus Christ the same yesterday, and today, and forever.' Heb. 13:8."

*   *   *   *   *

We received a letter at that time from W. Buchanan, a Christian worker at Melbourne, concerning the Wigglesworth campaign in that city: "We had three glorious weeks of triumphant victory in the Melbourne meetings. Fully one thousand souls were converted to the Lord Jesus Christ, and many scores were healed. In fact, the testimonies of those healed are still continuing to come in."

After being a great blessing in many parts of Australia, our Greatheart moved on to New Zealand. The following is a letter that was received from E. E. Pennington, Chairman of the New Zealand Evangelical Mission of Wellington: "In June, 1922, Smith Wigglesworth came to Wellington little known to any of us. There was no flourishing of trumpets to herald his advent—a few small advertisements in the local press announced his meetings. About one thousand attended his first meeting on Sunday evening, and the night following this number was increased by about five hundred to six hundred. From then on it was impossible to secure buildings large enough to accommodate the crowds; and the large Town Hall, seating three thousand, was packed every evening. On some occasions the crowd waited for hours about the doors before the commencement of the meetings rather than be denied the opportunity of hearing the man and his message. Never had the writer witnessed such scenes as followed the presentation of the Word of God by this Spirit-filled man, although he has been associated with such mighty evangelists as Torrey, Chapman, and others in part of their New Zealand campaigns. On every occasion when an appeal was made for the unconverted to decide for Christ, the response was immediate and great, sometimes as many as four hundred to five hundred responding in a meeting. Over two thousand made the great decision during the mission in Wellington—in some cases whole families entered the kingdom of God."

Some newspaper reports were not very friendly. We have before us, however, a special write-up which appeared in one newspaper under the heading, "Do You Believe in Faith Healing?" The article begins: "Of course you don't. That is to say, you don't believe in what you have never seen. But perhaps you have seen and been puzzled as I have been. Then again, perhaps you have seen and not been puzzled, but, instead, have been converted. A good many have been converted in Wellington recently. Some went with open minds; some did not, but went to scoff—and remained to pray.

"Whether you believe or you don't believe, the subject of faith healing is one of intense interest. Witness the thousands who assembled to hear and see Mr. Smith Wigglesworth at the Town Hall. The interest thus evidenced encouraged me to follow the matter up a little . . .

"I have before me a number of affidavits. They are those of Wellington citizens who presented themselves for healing before Mr. Smith Wigglesworth on his recent visit here. The affidavits are genuine; they were sworn before Mr. C. A. Baker, J. P., and they speak for themselves . . . I have omitted the names, but the originals were left for inspection at *The Dominion* office as a guarantee of their genuineness."

Then there follow five affidavits. The first is that of a dairyman who had suffered from chronic gastritis and paralysis of both legs from the hips downwards, and could only drag along with crutches. When the evangelist, after anointing him with oil, asked for his crutches, he gave them to him and walked home. He states that for fourteen years he had a cyst on the back of his neck and had often spoken to doctors about removing it. It was the size of an ordinary hen's egg. The morning after his healing, when he awoke he found that the cyst had completely disappeared.

One of these testimonies is from a girl twenty years of age, who since infancy had suffered from double curvature of the spine. She could not walk till she was four years of age and could never rise off the floor without pulling herself up with both hands. One leg was three inches shorter than the other and was almost useless, being three inches less in circumference than the other. She persuaded her parents to take her to the Town Hall. There the evangelist placed his hands on her head and on her spine, and she was instantly healed. "My spine was straightened, and in a few days my leg lengthened.

My hip which was diseased is well also. The Sunday following my healing I was so eager to attend the Mission that, as there was no train, I walked all the way from Ngalo to the Hall and back and felt no ill effect whatever."

After giving the five testimonies the reporter says: "There are several other affidavits of a similar nature, but space will not permit of their publication. Now what do you think of it? Do you believe in faith healing? Or are you still in the ranks of the skeptics?"

In 1927 our Greatheart was back in Australia and New Zealand. This time his daughter Alice—Mrs. James Salter—accompanied him. He held fruitful campaigns in a great many cities. The Word was confirmed with signs following. The two following remarkable stories speak for themselves. They both appeared in the *Australian Evangel* of April 1, 1927.

Nurse Tells of Healing

Miss H. Todd of Naremburn, N.S.W., testified: "While engaged in my occupation as nurse in Sydney I met with a serious accident, fracturing the knee cap and displacing the internal cartilage, which resulted in synovitis and arthritis (chronic). I had the best medical skill both in Sydney and Orange without any permanent relief. I was just up for a while and then back to bed again, and so on for eighteen months; and long, weary months they were, especially when, after about fourteen months, I had the misfortune to rupture the fibers of the muscles of the other leg, which resulted in having a layup for six weeks. The pain at times was most severe. I was a real invalid with no prospect of ever being able to follow my profession again. Being otherwise perfectly healthy, it was hard to look into the future with both legs crippled, to be dependent upon others to look after and keep me.

"How blind I was, for since being invalided to

Orange I had lived among folk who believed and tried to get me to listen to the Scriptural teaching of divine healing, but I thought differently. Truly the Bible did tell of wonderful things in bygone days, but to me those days were gone and things were different now. There was great talk of Evangelist Smith Wigglesworth, but I was not interested. After the evangelist had begun his mission, which would only last five days, my brother, together with others, spoke most convincingly to me about the reality of the teaching of the Scriptures on divine healing, and though I had been adverse to it right up till then, I went to my Bible again and, being like the prodigal son, at the end of myself, I too was led to say, 'I will arise and go to my Father.' And, praise the dear Lord, what blessings He had waiting to bestow upon me. I had been a Christian many years, but I had to be awakened before I could hear His voice and have Him anoint my eyes. While reading the Scripture I was arrested by the words, 'One thing I know, that, whereas I was blind, now I see.' John 9:25. This kept running through my mind all day Friday and Saturday; also the words of God, 'I am the Lord, I change not.' So persistently did these scriptures keep coming to me that I made up my mind to go that night to the mission for prayer.

"On one leg I had a steel and leather apparatus to keep the knee joint from locking and pinching, which caused intense pain, and the other was in tight bandages. With the aid of a pair of crutches I got out to the car to be taken to the meeting, and though suffering intensely, I believed I would be healed. After the address I joined with those who were to be ministered to, and as the evangelist laid his hands on me and prayed I had a strange yet beautiful experience as though cold water with great force was being sprayed in jets upon both of my afflicted members where they were injured. So strong seemed to be the force that it even hurt me, and I knew it was the Lord, but on turning to go away I didn't feel any better, and expressed disappointment to two or three.

"All the way home I wept copiously, and poured out my heart to God, and continued to say, 'Lord, I believe, help Thou my unbelief.' Arriving home, I was helped out of the car, and after walking a few steps, said that I thought I could walk alone. Just as I reached the threshold of the door, a wall of bright shining light confronted me, so exceedingly bright that it almost staggered me, and instantly I cried out, 'Glory to God, I'm healed,' and truly I was. I went through the house praising the Lord, and up and down the back verandah, glorifying God and walking as I did before meeting with the accident. Seeing the crutches, I said, 'Take those back to the kind friend that loaned them to me. I shall not want them any more.' So the crutches were returned just before midnight. Hallelujah! On rising next morning I discarded the steel and leather support and the bandages, and have never touched them since, for I was made every whit whole.

"Two days later I was sweetly baptized in the Holy Spirit according to Acts 2:4. My Bible means more to me now than ever before. I now see my Lord as my Savior from sin, the Great Physician, the One who baptizes with the Holy Ghost, and the One who is coming for His bride very soon."

Heart Patient Tells of Healing

The other testimony is from Mrs. M. Legate Pople, Orange N.S.W.: "Genesis 24:27—'I being in the way, the Lord led me'—seems to be the best explanation of God's wondrous blessings to me five weeks ago. How I did want to go home! My poor heart was in such a state, past all human aid; even the casing was ruptured so that the least move would cause a lump to protrude like an egg. For sixteen weeks I just lay prostrate, and how lovely it was to feel so near home, so often almost through the pearly gates; how real the dawning of that eternal day was to me, and how I just longed to enter right in. I was so bent on going 'home to glory' that when asked if I would like to have Evangelist Wigglesworth pray for me if I should be here when he came, I said an emphatic 'No,' and I certainly meant it. Such a band of dear friends were praying for me everywhere that I just felt I wanted no more; my mind and my hopes were all centered on things above and not on things here below. How little did I know what wondrous blessings there were here below that I had not even tasted of, that my dear loving Savior wanted me to experience before I should pass through the pearly gates, and how graciously did He work to bring it to pass.

"Brother Wigglesworth was not expected here for nearly two months, when suddenly dates were altered and he arrived almost without warning. Of course, this did not concern me, for my fellow invalid, Sister Todd" (whose testimony is also given in this chapter) "and I had made up our minds that we weren't going to have anything to do with the mission of the evangelist. How true are the Lord's words, 'My thoughts are not your thoughts, neither are your ways My ways, saith the Lord.' Isa. 55:8-11. As the mission went on, my friend, who was adverse to the teaching of Divine Healing, began to search the Scriptures afresh to see if these things that were being taught, and which were confidently affirmed by numbers around who believed, were so. She became so convinced of the truth of God, who said, 'I am the Lord; I change not,' that she came into my room saying she intended going to the mission for the laying on of hands and prayer.

"That night I saw her making her way out on her crutches to the car in great agony, and somehow I felt in myself that she would be healed. After her return she came skipping down the steps to my room, like the man of old leaping and praising God, and saying, 'Sister, I'm healed, I'm healed,' and so she was, perfectly and completely. Hallelujah! It was wonderful.

"All that night I prayed and sought the Lord, and then came the thought—how could I face my dear Lord whom I loved with all my heart if I just slipped home, having refused to prove whether He wanted me to do any more 'little corner filling' for Him, when before my eyes He had wrought such a miracle?

"In the morning, the closing day of the mission, I was waiting for someone to come down to my room, to ask them if they would take a message to Brother Wigglesworth and see if he would come and pray for me after the morning service. After breakfast I could hear the dear ones of the house holding a prayer meeting, but as they had closed the door I could not hear what was taking place. How I was longing for someone to come in to take my message, but no; time was getting away, and how I pleaded with the Lord. Could it be that they were all too much occupied with their own blessings and were unmindful of me? I questioned. Ah no, but because I had said 'No' so decisively they would not ask me again, and they were all asking the Lord to constrain me to ask for prayer.

"Presently different ones came into my room but did not look at me or give me the usual smile and kind word. I asked each if they would take my message, and not until I had made the request five times did I get a promise that they would. I had said 'No' once but had to say 'Yes' five times. How long it seemed before that morning service was over; but at last, in came the matron, face beaming, and said, 'He's come.' I vaguely remember seeing a man step into the room, and after that saw no man but Jesus only. How sweetly does the dear Lord manifest Himself. The evangelist told his daughter (Mrs. Salter) to put her hands on my knees, and he put his on my head and prayed a wonderful prayer (wonderful to me because I was right in glory). Then he laid his hands on my heart and prayed for my healing, at the same time rebuking death and commanding it to be dashed away in Jesus' name.

"When he first came in he said, 'Are you ready to get

up?' I said, 'Yes, I am,' and now he said, 'Get up,' and up I got. My inability to even move just a few minutes before was entirely forgotten. One thought only seemed to possess me, and that was to get dressed as quickly as possible. I rushed across the floor and lifted down two heavy suitcases filled with books in order to get to where I could find some clothing. I was in such a hurry, I wanted to be dressed ready to greet 'my girls' of my Bible class who used to flock in after church just to have a peep at me. In the afternoon before I had lain semi-conscious for hours, and those who saw me then thought perhaps it was the last look; and here I was trying to find clothes to let them see me every whit whole! I was just ready when the door opened and a number of them were admitted, and what a shock they got. Some wept; some laughed, then wept; they hugged me, then would think of my heart and let go; but it was all right. I was healed perfectly and completely, and felt no weakness after my sixteen weeks in bed, when I had eaten scarcely anything. All the while I had lain there I was neither hungry nor thirsty, and would take little sips just to oblige those who brought it to me. Now I wanted my dinner, and a good dinner I had. I was changed, a new creation, just filled with God, divinely healed, raised up in a moment, from the shadow of death to abounding life—saved to serve.

"The day following my healing I was gloriously baptized in the Holy Spirit according to Acts 2:4, and daily and hourly He fills me with joy unspeakable and full of glory."

IX

VISITS TO SWITZERLAND
AND SWEDEN

~~~~~~

IN THE year 1920 our Greatheart labored for six months in different parts of Europe. He ministered for a short while in France and then went on to Switzerland. The following account of his labors is part of an address given by Madame Debat of Paris, who acted as his interpreter in France and in French Switzerland.

Madame Debat's Report

At Chartres in the French Alps we had a convention. Four ministers came to spy out the land in order to speak against this work of God. But all four are now convinced that this Pentecostal work is truly of God. One cried out, "I am under an open heaven."

A wagon drawn by oxen drew up at the meeting house, containing a man on a stretcher who had come some distance with faith to be healed. He was suffering with cancer of the stomach and could not eat. In the wagon was a basket of provisions. He was asked what they were for, as he could not eat anything. He replied, "No, I cannot eat, but I am going to be healed and I shall consume these provisions on the return journey." He had simple faith, and of course God met him.

I asked one woman going out of the meeting, "Are you healed?" She replied, "Of course I am healed." There were several cases of deafness healed. In one case the bone had been scraped and the drum disappeared, but she heard perfectly.

At Lausanne was a man born blind. His wife was tubercular and in a terrible condition. She heard of the meetings and she asked her husband if he could exercise faith for healing. He answered her sarcastically and with obvious unbelief. But they came to the meeting and both were saved, healed and baptized. Their very countenances changed, for the woman had previously had a terribly hard face. The man's case is a case of slow recovery, but his eyesight is coming little by little. There was another man suffering from deafness and rupture. He thought he could not ask for deliverance from two things so asked for the deafness to go. He was healed of both his troubles. There was a child who had a new eye given to him; also a woman nearly blind was healed; also there were numbers of cases of lame people who left their sticks behind.

At Godivil, three were healed of consumption, one a girl of nineteen who was in a dying condition and having severe hemorrhages. God has greatly blessed her. She has received the Baptism and gives such a sweet testimony.

At Vevey there was a brother named Zand. He was always hungry and thirsty after God and going wherever he thought he could learn more of Him. He was among the Open Brethren. He said, "I am not satisfied that I have received the baptism of the Holy Spirit at conversion—I lack something." When he made this statement his brethren thought he was a heretic and told him to clear out. He said, "That is what I am going to do." He came and was baptized in the Spirit. Here there is a band of fine young men and they have good open-air meetings. Four of them went up the mountain and began to pray. Some passers-by began to stone them. They went deeper into the wood and prayed until morning, all four receiving the baptism in the Holy Spirit.

At Morges we had a convention. A man was brought in a wheelchair who had not walked for several years. His healing was just like that of the man at the Beautiful Gate. He leaped and jumped, and he walked home followed by a boy wheeling the chair, and a crowd of boys who all knew that he had been healed. Another was healed of a nervous breakdown. He went to a doctor who told him to go and return thanks because he was cured. At Geneva three hundred came out for salvation. God blessed in a similar way in the part of Switzerland where German is spoken.

At Neuchatel, God marvelously moved. One who had a wonderful Baptism repeated all the Sermon on the Mount. Another, under the inspiration of the Spirit, spoke Italian and German, whereas French is the language spoken in Neuchatel.

*   *   *   *   *

Speaking of his visit to Switzerland, our Greatheart says that it was wonderful to see the Spirit of God brooding over the people as he spoke through an interpreter. A woman with a cancer on her nose and the upper part of her face, came forward to be prayed with. He had her stand right in front of the people and said to them, "Look at her. She will be here tomorrow night and you will see what God has done for her." He prayed for her and she left the meeting. The next night she came back, and it was seen that the cancer had gone and there was a new skin on her face.

There was another case of a woman whose face was in a terrible condition through some disease she had contracted. She was prayed for and the next day she appeared with an entirely new skin, and she had a radiant complexion.

A young man came to the meeting to ridicule, but he was stricken down and could not speak. Wigglesworth commanded the evil spirit to come out of him and he was loosed. At another meeting three insane people were sent and put in the front row with a view to creating a disturbance. Wigglesworth, in the name of Jesus, commanded the demons to keep quiet and there was no further trouble.

A child was brought to one meeting very sick. The doctors said the sickness had to do with the head. The evangelist was shown by the Spirit that the trouble was in the stomach. As he laid hands on the stomach and prayed, a worm, sixteen inches long, came out of the child's mouth.

One day when he was in Switzerland two policemen were sent to arrest him on a warrant that he was healing the people without a license. They went to the house of the minister of a Pentecostal Assembly of Godivil. He said to them: "Mr. Wigglesworth is away just now, but before you arrest him I would like to show you one result of his ministry in this place." He took the two policemen down to the lowest quarter in the town to the house of a woman whom they had arrested time and time again for drunken brawls, a woman who spent most of her time behind prison walls. This minister said: "This woman came to one of our meetings in a state of drunkenness. While she was there in this condition Mr. Wigglesworth laid his hands on her and asked God to deliver her. Her body was broken out in two places with terrible sores, but God has healed her and delivered her from drunkenness." The woman spoke for herself and said to the policemen, "God saved my soul at that time, and from that moment I have not had the slightest desire for liquor." The police officers said, "We refuse to stop this kind of work. Somebody else will have to arrest this man." And nothing further came of it.

One day, in the city of Neuchatel, a dentist, Dr. Emil Lanz, came to the meeting. He thought in his heart, "I believe this man is a fake. He is preaching divine healing, and yet he probably has a set of artificial teeth. After the meeting I will go up to him and ask him to open his mouth. If his teeth are artificial I will expose him as a deceiver." So at the end of the meeting, this dentist asked Wigglesworth to open his mouth for him to look at his teeth. He was amazed, as he later testified, to see the most perfect set of teeth that he had ever seen in anyone's mouth. Smith Wigglesworth had faith in God that He would keep every one of his teeth, and the Lord preserved them so that he had all his own teeth at eighty-seven years of age.

Dr. Lanz was convinced and began to trust the Lord himself. Some years later, speaking in London, he said, "We have seen great things in Switzerland in the past three years, and many new gatherings have been raised up in both French and German Switzerland through the ministry of Mr. Smith Wigglesworth. Many, many of our people have received the great Pentecostal blessing of the Baptism of the blessed Holy Ghost with signs following, and we are deeply grateful for this. Two years ago in Berne, we had only fifteen to twenty coming to the meetings. Today we have a great gathering and a beautiful hall. The young folk meet in the open air and preach the glad tidings of deliverance from sin and the baptism in the Holy Ghost. Every Sunday night there is a great open-air meeting in the center of the town, many have been saved, and healed, and baptized in the Holy Ghost."

Mr. Wigglesworth told us, "In Switzerland I was put into prison twice. But praise God, I was brought out all right. One officer said to me, 'I find no fault with you. You have been a great blessing to us here in Switzerland.' In the middle of one night they said to me, 'You can go.' I said, 'No, I'll only go on one condition, that every officer in this place gets down on his knees and I'll pray for you.'"

A woman in Neuchatel had suffered with tumors in the kidneys for many years. She had had many doctors but they gave her no permanent relief. She went to a hospital in Berne to be operated upon, but the doctors found seven tumors and said it was impossible to operate. She heard of the meetings and came to be ministered to. She fully recovered and was baptized in the Holy Spirit. She had the joy of giving her son (who was saved in the meetings and called of God) to go to the mission field in Congo Belge in Africa.

A Danish lady, Madame Lewini, who had formerly graced the stage in Denmark, but later became a missionary, writes of being with Wigglesworth in three months of campaigns in Sweden and Denmark. This is her record.

Madame Lewini Tells of God's Blessings in Sweden and Denmark

"It was a time of visitation from on high. I dare to say that hundreds of people received Jesus as their Savior, thousands were healed of all kinds of diseases, also thousands of people awoke to a new life and many received the baptism of the Holy Spirit as on the Day of Pentecost. For all this we give glory to Jesus. Here are a few examples of miracles my eyes have seen.

"I will begin with the first meeting I attended. It was in Orebro, Sweden. I came to seek help for myself, being worn out by long unbroken service in the Lord's work. On the second day there was a meeting for healing. After the preaching service hundreds of men and women came for a touch of God, and glory to God, we were not disappointed. As hands were laid upon me the power of God went through me in a wonderful way. I was immediately healed.

"It was wonderful to notice, as the ministry continued, the effect upon the people as the power of the Lord came over them. Some lifted their hands crying, 'I am

healed! I am healed!' Some fell on the platform, over-
powered by the power of the Spirit, and had to be
helped down. A young blind girl, as she was ministered
to, cried out, 'Oh, how many windows there are in this
hall!' During the three weeks the meetings continued
the great chapel was crowded daily, multitudes being
healed and many saved. The testimony meetings were
wonderful. One said, 'I was deaf; they prayed, and
Jesus healed me.' Another, 'I had consumption, and I
am free.' And so on.

"At Skovde a smaller hall was set apart for those
seeking the baptism of the Holy Spirit. Did the Holy
Spirit fall upon them? Of course He did. Here also
many were healed. There was a young man whose body
was spoiled because of sin, but the Lord is merciful with
sinners. He was anointed, and when hands were laid
upon him the power of God went marvelously over him.
He cried, 'I am healed.' He broke down and cried like a
little child as he confessed his sin. At the same moment
God saved him. He went into the large hall and testified
that the Lord had saved him and healed him.

"At Stockholm at nearly every meeting the crowds
were unable to enter the building, but they waited often
hour on hour for a chance, if any left the building, to
step into the place. Here a man with two crutches, his
whole body shaking with palsy, was lifted on to the
platform. He was anointed and hands were laid upon
him in the name of Jesus. He continued to shake. Then
he dropped one crutch, and after a short while the other
one. His body still shook but he took the first step out *in
faith*. He lifted one foot and then the other and walked
around the platform. Then he walked around the auditorium.

"During this meeting a woman began to shout and
shout. The preacher told her to be quiet, but instead she
jumped on a chair, flourishing her arms about, and
cried, 'I am healed! I had cancer in my mouth, and I
was unsaved. But during this meeting as I listened to the
Word of God, the Lord has saved me and healed me of

cancer of the mouth.' She was quite beside herself. The people laughed and cried together.

"Here was another woman unable to walk, sitting on a chair as she was ministered to. Her experience was the same as hundreds of the others. She rose up, looking around, wondering if after all it was a dream. Suddenly she laughed and said, 'My leg is healed!' Afterwards she said, 'I am not saved,' and streams of tears ran down her face. They prayed for her and later she left the meeting healed and saved and full of joy.

"In Christiania (now Oslo) a man and his son came in a taxi to a meeting. Both had crutches. The father had been in bed two years and was unable to put his leg to the ground. He was ministered to. He dropped both crutches, walked and praised God. When the son saw this he cried out, 'Help me too,' and after a little while father and son, without crutches and without taxi walked away from the hall together.

"At Copenhagen thousands daily attended the meetings. Each morning two or three hundred were ministered to for healing. Each evening the platform was surrounded. Again and again, as each throng retired, another company came forward seeking salvation. Here many were baptized in the Holy Spirit. The testimony meetings were wonderful."

* * * * *

Our Greatheart wrote a letter from Christiania of the great crowds that flocked to the meetings. Thousands could not get in the large buildings that were taken for the campaign. He said:

"I ministered for over three hours to the sick, after preaching an hour and a half. Many coming were helpless. Hundreds were healed. A great pile of crutches and sticks and other helps have been left on the large platform. I ministered openly and the crowds looked on and shouted. The excitement was wonderful as the blind saw and the lame leaped. We are now in a place holding

5000 and the people say it will be too small. One man was in the hospital and asked permission to go to the meetings, and was refused. Then he decided to go and the doctors said, 'If you go, you will not come back.' The man said, 'No, I shall not come back.' After prayer, he was instantly healed and threw his crutches away. I tell you the thing is great, and greater things are ahead for us—only believe."

Speaking afterwards of his work in Sweden Mr. Wigglesworth said, "When I was in Sweden the power of God was mightily upon me. It was there that I was apprehended for preaching and for praying for the sick. The Lutheran churches and the doctors rose up like an army against me, and had special audience with the king to try to get me out of the country. It was in Sweden that I was escorted out by two detectives and two policemen, because of the mighty power of God moving among the people. But beloved, it was lovely!

"One of the nurses in the king's household came and was healed of a leg trouble—I forget whether a broken thigh or a dislocated joint. She went to the king and said, 'I have been so wonderfully healed by this man. You know I am walking all right now.' 'Yes,' said the king, 'I know everything about him. Tell him to go. I do not want him turned out. If he goes out, he can come back; but if he is turned out he cannot come back.' I thank God I was not turned out, I was merely escorted out.

"The Pentecostal people went to see the police to see if I could have a big meeting in the park on the Monday following Whitsunday (the anniversary of Pentecost). The police officers said: 'There is only one reason why we could refuse him and it is on this line. If that man puts his hand upon the sick in the great park, it would take thirty more policemen to guard the situation. But if he will promise us that he will not lay his hands upon the people, then we will allow you to have the park.'

"They came and asked me and I said, 'Promise them that I will fulfill their wishes.' I knew that God was not limited to my laying hands on the people. When the presence of the Lord is there to heal it does not require the laying on of hands. Faith is the great operating factor. When we *believe God,* all things are easy.

"They built a platform where I could speak to thousands of people. I prayed and said, 'Lord, you know the situation. You have never yet been in a fix where you could not handle the situation. Show me what can be done for this poor and needy people without having hands laid upon them. Show me.'

"To the people I said, 'All of you that would like the power of God to go through you today healing everything, put your hands up.' Thousands of hands went up. I sent up a cry, 'Oh, Lord, show me,' and He told me as clearly as anything to pick a person out that stood upon a rock. That park was a very rocky place. I told them to put their hands down except this person. To her I said, 'Tell all the people what are your troubles.' She began to relate her troubles. From her head to her feet she was so in pain that she felt if she did not sit down or lie down she would not be able to go on.

"I said to her, 'Lift your hands high.' I then said, 'In the name of Jesus I rebuke the evil one from your head to your feet, and I believe God has loosed you.' Oh, how she danced and how she jumped and how she shouted!

"That was the first time that God revealed to me that it was a very simple matter for Him to heal without the laying on of my hands. I said to the sick people, 'Now each one lay hands on yourself, and when I pray God will heal you.' We had hundreds healed that day without my touching them and hundreds were saved. Our God is a God of mighty power. Oh, how wonderful, how glorious, and how fascinating it is that we can come into this royal palace of faith and of power. We have a great God. We have a wonderful Jesus. I believe in the Holy Ghost."

X

HIS SECRET OF SPIRITUAL STRENGTH

~~~~~~~~~~~~~~~~~~~~~~~~~~~~~~~~~~~

MANY WILL ask, "Had Smith Wigglesworth any spiritual secret? Wherein did his great strength lie?" The two main factors in his spiritual life were these: his reliance upon the Spirit of God and his confidence in the Word of God. These were the foundations of his holy audacity and his constant boldness of action.

He was preeminently a man of the Word just as he was preeminently a man of the Spirit. He declared, "Libraries make swelled heads, but the Word of God makes enlarged hearts. We are to have enlarged hearts, hearts filled with the fragrance of the love of God that will show forth the life and power of the Lord."

He said, "Faith cometh by hearing, and hearing by the Word of God—not by reading commentaries. Faith is the principle of the Word of God. The Holy Spirit, who inspired the Word, is called the Spirit of truth; and as we receive with meekness the engrafted Word, faith springs up in our hearts; faith in the sacrifice of Calvary; faith in the shed blood of Jesus; faith in the fact that He took our weaknesses upon Himself, that He has borne our sicknesses and carried our pains, and that He is our life today. The Word of God is living and powerful, and in its treasure you will find eternal life. If you will dare to trust this wonderful Lord of life, you will find in Him everything you need."

He frequently said, "I have never read any book but the Bible." A critic who heard him say this, wrote saying, "How is it that this man who says he has read no book but the Bible has been guilty of writing a book? for we see his book, *Ever Increasing Faith* advertised in the columns of *The Pentecostal Evangel*." We wrote back to that good man and said, "Smith Wigglesworth was not guilty of writing that book. It came into existence in this way: He came to Springfield, Missouri, in 1923, in the early days of Central Bible Institute. Each morning he talked to the students and each night he spoke to a large crowd at the Convention Hall. We took down these messages for *The Pentecostal Evangel,* and after they had appeared in that paper we asked the printers to hold the type. When sufficient messages were ready, we put them into a book. Smith Wigglesworth did not even read the copy." We are conscious that there are crudities in the book but nevertheless God owned it and has made it a blessing to the salvation and healing of a great many the world over.*

The prophet Ezekiel received the word of the Lord: "Open thy mouth, and eat that I give thee." He tells us, "When I looked, behold, an hand was sent unto me, and lo, a roll of a book was therein." The Lord commanded, "Son of man, eat that thou findest; eat this roll, and go speak." And the prophet said, "So I opened my mouth, and He caused me to eat that roll." Again the Lord said, "Son of man, cause thy belly to eat, and fill thy bowels with this roll that I give thee."

Our Greatheart was continually eating the "roll," and it was made alive in his inner being; so he would go and

---

Ever Increasing Faith is published by the Gospel Publishing House, Springfield, Mo.

speak with authority and faith to those to whom God sent him. His son-in-law, James Salter, who was very often traveling with him, says: "He was essentially a man of the Bible, and he never considered himself fully dressed without a copy of the Word of God in his pocket. He not only carried it, but he used it continually. While others might read novels or newspapers in railway cars, he read his Bible. On board various ships as he traveled, at the seaside where occasionally he went for relaxation, or sitting in his favorite place in the park near his home, his New Testament was constantly in his hand. He never left a friend's table without reading 'a bit from the Book,' and usually his comments on it were choicer than any course in the meal."

His constant advice to young people was, "Fill your head and your heart with the Scriptures. Memorize passages from the Word, with the name of the book, the chapter, and the verse, so that you can quote the scripture correctly in addresses or in open-air meetings. As you do this, you are sowing in your heart seeds which the Spirit of God can germinate. He can bring to your remembrance from time to time that which you have once memorized. You must be so *soaked* with the Word of God, you must be so *filled* with it, that you yourself are a living epistle, known and read of all men. Believers are strong only as the Word of God abides in them. The Word of God is spirit and life to those who receive it in simple faith, and it is a vivifier of all who own its sway. Know your Book, live it, believe it, and obey it. Hide God's Word in your heart. It will save your soul, quicken your body, and illumine your mind. The Word of God is full and final, infallible, reliable, and up-to-date, and our attitude towards it must be one of unquestioned obedience. If a thing is in the Bible it is so; it is not even to be prayed about; it is to be received and acted upon. Inactivity of faith is a robber which steals blessing. Increase comes by action, by using what we have and what we know. Your life must be one of going from faith to faith."

He constantly taught that the Word of God must be implicitly obeyed. He repeatedly quoted the scripture, "To obey is better than sacrifice." Obedience, to him, was a normal fruit of true faith. "Because you dare to believe, you act in obedience."

In addition to taking time each day to read the Word of God, our Greatheart learned the secret of often turning aside from the multitude and getting alone with God for a spiritual renewing. He became acquainted with a very godly minister who was one time visiting England and who carried with him an unusual degree of the presence of God. His preaching was plain and unadorned, but he took his hearers into conscious contact with the Lord. Many zealous souls sought to learn the secret of his power, but he was reluctant to tell them. However, after he had prayed about the matter, the Lord gave him liberty to tell those who inquired the secret of his deep spiritual ministry. He said, "Years ago the Spirit of God began to speak to me, but I was too busy to heed His voice. He persisted, until I commenced to go aside when He spoke, so that I could hear what God the Lord had to say. This became my manner of life. I obeyed His pleading voice; until now, at the slightest breath of the Spirit, I leave everyone and everything to be in His presence, to hear and to obey His Word."

Our Greatheart caught the vision of this godly minister, and with the Word of God in his hand he could be "otherwise engaged," completely shut in with God alone, in any crowd or company. His secret may have been a borrowed one, but it is now an open one to every devoted servant of God.

One day he was traveling in a railroad car when a mother and her daughter were both stricken ill. He told them that he had in his bag a remedy for every trouble and that it never failed in the worst cases; in fact, it had never been known to fail where the conditions were met. He talked so much about what he had in his bag that they pleaded for a dose of this wonderful universal remedy. He opened his bag, took out his Bible and read the scripture, "I am the Lord that healeth thee." And he prayed that they might have faith in this wonderful Healer. In a short while both declared that they were healed.

One time in the city of Cardiff in South Wales he prayed for a woman who was instantly healed. She came to the next meeting and testified with great joy to what the Lord had done for her. She said that she wanted to spread the truth that had been so beneficial to her, and asked our Greatheart for some tracts. He answered, "The best tracts I know of on healing are Matthew, Mark, Luke, and John. They are full of incidents of the power and working of Jesus Christ. He is the same yesterday, and today, and forever. You cannot have anything better."

One time he prayed for a young man who was sick. After he had prayed, the young man said: "Brother, I want a promise to stand on." Wigglesworth put his Bible on the ground and said to the young man, "Now stand on that." He stood on it and was told, "Now you are standing on a great heap of promises. Believe every one of them."

Previous to the year 1907, the year he received the Pentecostal Baptism, the Holy Spirit figured constantly in his experience and teaching, but from that time forward a new epoch began in his life. He relied implicitly upon the Holy Spirit for every phase of his ministry. He certainly sought to live in the Spirit and to be led by the Spirit. The gift of tongues was a priceless treasure to him and many times every day his heart went out in love and adoration to God, not in the defiled languages of earth, but in the Holy-Spirit-given language of love that God had graciously given him. He found that this speaking in tongues was always a source of spiritual edification. He lived that verse in Jude 20, "Beloved, building up yourselves in your most holy faith, *praying in the Holy Ghost,*" and he also lived that verse, "Praying always with all prayer and supplication in the Spirit, and watching thereunto with all perseverance and supplication for all saints."

James Salter says of his preaching: "How often, metaphorically speaking, he built up the altar of God and got ready to sacrifice; and then God sent the fire and consumed the offering, thus consummating his efforts. He certainly searched the Scriptures, and prayed day and night to show himself approved unto God, a workman that needeth not to be ashamed, rightly dividing the Word of truth. But it was the breath of God, the unction from heaven, and the person and power of the Holy Spirit that made him what he was. He knew it, and jealously guarded this deposit." We have heard him say, "I am nothing apart from the Holy Spirit," and he certainly was not.

Another secret of his power was that he was constantly "moved with compassion." He saw that the source of Christ's mightiest miracles was His wonderful compassion. Tears would stream from his eyes as he beheld the sin-scarred souls and the sickness-wrecked bodies. He burned in his zeal to undo the works of the devil, and was positively aggressive as he tried to emulate his Master in going about doing good, and healing all that were oppressed of the devil.

One who knew him intimately wrote of him: "When the mail arrived at his home and the time for the opening of the letters came, we all had to stop whatever we were doing and get under the burden. There was nothing rushed or slipshod about his methods of dealing with these pathetic appeals for help. Everybody in the house must join in the prayers and lay lands on the handkerchiefs sent out to the suffering ones. They were treated as though the writers were present in person. Each request was dealt with separately and sincerely, and thousands of grateful people all over the world testified to the outcome of this compassionate ministry.

"One day the mail brought him quite a long letter from a lady who was suffering intensely from a serious disease. Her letter was full of quotations on the subject of divine healing, and showed that she knew all that she needed to know on that subject. He read the letter a time or two, and then he passed it on to me, saying, 'What do you think of that?' He reread it, and then wrote on the bottom of the letter: 'Believe your own letter, apply it to your own body like a handkerchief, and you will be healed.' He sent it back to her, and a short time later he received a letter from her saying that she was perfectly whole."

XI

THE CHALLENGER

〜〜〜〜〜〜〜〜〜〜〜〜〜〜〜〜

THERE USED to be a daily train from Chicago to California named *The Challenger*. "The Challenger" would have been an excellent name for Smith Wigglesworth.

Frequently he would begin his preaching by sending out the challenge: "Are you ready? What for? Ready to believe God! Ready to catch the vision of what God has for you! Ready to enter right into God's plan for you today!"

For himself, he was always Wigglesworth the everready.

Paul sent a letter to the citadel of the Caesars, declaring: "I am ready to preach the gospel to you that are at Rome also." Romans 1:15. One day Wigglesworth made a trip to the city of Rome, and he was ready to preach there. On the street he met an Italian brother who had heard him preach in California. This man took him to where the Pentecostal saints worshiped in Rome, and there it was his joy to minister Christ.

He later visited the city of Rome with Mr. and Mrs.

Salter to hold special meetings there, and one day it was decided to pay a visit to the catacombs. A special young English-speaking priest was allocated to be their guide. They were each given a thick wax taper to light their way underground. The priest seemed to forget the rest of the party, but took a special interest in Smith Wigglesworth, who was intensely interested in all that he saw and heard. Repeatedly the priest would say to him, "You would make a good Catholic. You ought to be a Catholic;" and each time he would answer: "I am a Catholic, but not a Roman Catholic."

The priest continued speaking with Wigglesworth until the end of the tour and the time came for them to ascend the steps and leave the catacombs. Then Smith Wigglesworth seized the opportunity and said to the priest: "Now, you would make a good Christian if you were to get saved. Kneel down here on the floor, and I will ask God to save you." The priest was astounded, burst into a flood of tears, and knelt down. Putting his hand on the man's head, Smith Wigglesworth prayed that God would save his soul. The priest kissed his hands most fervidly and it took Smith Wigglesworth some time to get free from his embrace.

One day, in Cardiff in Wales, a man who had a reputation for large-heartedness gathered together a large and representative group of Christian leaders. Unity and harmony were the themes of this convention, and emphasis was given to the need of the Holy Spirit and personal holiness.

As is the custom at many such gatherings, all the speakers dealt in general terms, none of them acute enough to hurt anyone's feelings. Everything seemed to be going very well, and the organizer beamed his satisfaction. But there was one man in that large audience who was stirred by the thought: "All these folk are missing God's best. Can I remain criminally silent and not tell this great audience that there is a mighty baptism in the Holy Spirit for everyone of them like that which the disciples received on the Day of Pentecost?"

And so that man, our courageous Greatheart, caused no small stir when he arose, took off his coat and came forward in his shirt-sleeves, and from the platform sent out this challenge: "If I had all you have now before I received *this,* what is this I have received since and in addition to all I had when I had all you have?"

Then he added: "I was saved among the Methodists when I was about eight years of age. A little later I was confirmed by a bishop of the Church of England. Later I was immersed as a Baptist. I had the grounding in Bible teaching among the Plymouth Brethren. I marched under the Blood and Fire banner of the Salvation Army, learning to win souls in the open air. I received the second blessing of sanctification and a clean heart under the teaching of Reader Harris and the Pentecostal League. I claimed the gift of the Holy Spirit by faith as I waited ten days before the Lord. But in Sunderland, in 1907, I knelt before God and had an Acts 2:4 experience. The Holy Spirit came and I spoke with new tongues as did the company in the upper room. That put my experience outside the range of argument, but inside the record of God's Holy Word. God gave me the Holy Spirit as He did to them at the beginning. I want harmony, unity and oneness, but I want them in God's way. In the Acts of the Apostles, speaking with new tongues was the sign of the infilling and outflowing of the Holy Spirit, and I do not believe that God has changed His method."

A tense atmosphere filled the building and the chairman hurriedly brought the meeting to a close. But Smith Wigglesworth had sent out his challenge. He felt that the Pentecostal testimony was worth standing for, and as always he fought a good fight, a fight for the distinctive testimony of the Pentecostal believers. He felt that the Pentecostal heritage must not be bartered for a mess of pottage. Then, as always, he fearlessly contended that the full Pentecostal baptism in the Spirit is invariably accompanied by the speaking with other tongues as the Spirit gives utterance.

He would constantly sound out the challenge: "Live ready. If you have to get ready when opportunity comes your way, you are too late. Opportunity does not wait, not even while you pray. You must not have to get ready; you must live ready."

On the occasion of his first visit to America, he heard of a camp meeting being held in Cazadero, in northern California, and he decided to attend. When he arrived he told Mr. and Mrs. Montgomery, who had convened the camp, who he was; and the first night, after several ministers had spoken, the one in charge of the meeting looked critically at Wigglesworth as he said, "Now it is your turn. Are you ready?" Wigglesworth smiled and replied, "Always." Taking off his coat, he advanced to the front of the platform, and before he had been speaking many minutes he had captivated his large audience by his unique message. From that day forward, he was asked to speak every morning and every night during the remaining three weeks of the camp, for the various invited speakers said: "This man has a message of faith that is outstanding and we want to hear him." At that camp meeting invitation after invitation was given to him to come and minister in various Californian cities.

Smith Wigglesworth would challenge his audience, "All who believe in prayer, put one hand up. All who believe in praying aloud, put two hands up. Now, everybody stand up and do it, and get what your heart desires." At the commencement, this method of procedure met with a mixed reception. Some tolerated it, but others openly opposed it. In the main, people obeyed and got much benefit. In conservative England there was not a little objection to his methods, but he was quite sure he was in harmony with the saints of the early church who "lifted up their voice to God with one accord." He would say, "This lifting up of holy hands is not something that Wigglesworth has invented. It is found in the first book of the Bible. Abraham did it. And in the last book of the Bible, we may read about the angel doing it.

Moses, Aaron, David, Jeremiah, Ezekiel—all did it. It meant all the difference between winning or losing a battle when Moses lifted up his hands to God against the Amalekites. In Hebrews we read, 'Lift up the hands which hang down.' In Psalm 134 the psalmist bids all the servants of the Lord, 'Lift up your hands in the sanctuary, and bless the Lord.' Paul echoes this in 1 Timothy 2:8, where he writes: 'I will therefore that men pray everywhere, lifting up holy hands, without wrath and doubting.' In the book of Nehemiah we have an example: 'And Ezra blessed the Lord, the great God. And all the people answered, Amen, Amen, with lifting up their hands; and they bowed their heads, and worshipped the Lord with their faces to the ground.' So you see we can go even a bit further and still be scriptural."

At the close of his services, he would frequently round up the audience with an appeal on this wise: "Now, who wants to get nearer to God? Who would like a special blessing? Let everybody who is hungry for God stand on his feet. Everybody who is in real earnest, move forward. If you move forward only a foot, it will show that you mean business. If you will come right up to the front, we will pray with you and God will meet you." The people would flock to the front. He would exhort them: "Who will lift up his hands in faith and ask God for something?" "Now thank God for it." "Now again, ask God for something." "Now thank God." The exercise of faith brought the answer to hundreds, and many were baptized in the Spirit as they lifted up their hands and voices to God.

At these after-meetings he adopted a definiteness and a conciseness that got folk further and got more for them in a minute than some ministers would have obtained in a millennium. He taught them that a definite faith brought a definite experience and a definite utterance. He instructed his hearers how to leap over obstacles and intermediate things, and get quickly and effectually to their goal and obtain their object.

His instructions to the seekers were usually very terse: "Ask for what you want; believe, receive from God, and thank God for it." "If you ask God seven times for the same thing, six times are in unbelief," was one of his sayings. "You can feel just how you feel any time you like to feel. Feelings are liars. Isaac felt Jacob, but he was cheated just the same. Faith is better than feelings, and if you have faith you will have all the feelings you can feel. When the woman with an issue of blood touched in faith the hem of His garment, she soon had plenty of feelings. She felt in her body that she was healed of that plague."

Although his life was a combination of incessant prayer and praise, and every word and work was an act of worship, he was not given to protracted periods of fasting and prayer. He practiced himself and encouraged his hearers to live a life of consistent confidence in God so that they were ready for any occasion and never taken unawares by any emergency. To him, Christ's words, "Only believe," meant *"Only* believe." Other methods of approach to God and getting things from God were of secondary importance to him. Yet he realized and sincerely appreciated the fact that his ministry was sustained largely by a host of people who would give themselves to the ministry of prayer, and in all his letters to such folk he pleaded for a continuance of their prayerful support.

"A preacher must not tell his audience what he thinks but what he knows, and let them do the thinking," he would say. He certainly set a lot of folk thinking whenever he arose to speak. He was not always as clear in his use of Bible terms as some folk wished he would be. Consequently, there were occasions when he was accused of teaching doctrines which were open to question. His use of the word "mortality" led some Christians to affirm that he taught the theory that there is no need to die. Actually, the champions of that teaching had no stronger opponent, as some of them could testify. Quoting Romans 8:11, he maintained that it was gloriously possible to know the surging resurrection life of Christ in the mortal body now, but none knew better than he that "the outward man perisheth."

His entrance into any meeting introduced a new element. The spiritual temperature would rise, and the expectancy of something different would fill the building. "Anyone can be ordinary," he would say, "but a person filled with the Holy Spirit must be extraordinary." The people looked to him for something new, something out of the usual run of things, and they were not disappointed.

He constantly talked about the power of faith in God. He would say, "Fear looks; faith jumps." "Faith never fails to obtain its object. If I leave you as I found you, I am not God's channel. I am not here to entertain you but to get you to the place where you can laugh at the impossible, to believe and to see the goodness of the Lord in the land of the living." "Men of faith always have a good report." "I am satisfied with the dissatisfaction that never rests until it is satisfied and satisfied again." "We have to get rid of our small measure because God's measure is so much greater than ours—a measure than cannot be measured."

Here are a few of his challenging assertions.

Favorite Wigglesworth Quotes

Far too many of us dwell on the lowlands of salvation. Can't you hear voices calling you to the uplands of divine grace? Mountain climbing is thrilling! Let's be off! Hebron's heights rise before us. Shall we explore our unclaimed inheritance in the heavenlies?

"Be filled with the Spirit," i.e., Be *soaked* with the Spirit; so soaked that every thread in the fabric of your life will have received the requisite hue of the Spirit. Then when you are misused and squeezed to the wall, all that will ooze out of you will be the Jesus nature.

The Knights of Pentecost—all they seek is a place of

service, and they care little about its being a place of honor; they aspire after travail rather than applause; if they can but be popular with the Supreme Potentate of their society, they ask nothing more.

We should be far more concerned about a rich and noble character than we are about a big reputation. Popularity can be bought almost any day for a song and sold for a sparrow, but a noble character is the product of years of divine training and discipline.

It is not poverty from which Christians suffer, but it is the disease called stinginess and selfishness; and hence, while they have enough and to spare for themselves, their children, and their pleasures, they lack the heart to give in order to promote God's glory and the good of their fellow-men.

Far too many people spend their entire lifetime making a living. Making a living is the small, time-serving, dwarfed and paralyzed man's object. Making a life is the kingly, righteous and holy man's object. The one lives in the narrow, prison-limited circle of self, and the other in a world which is bounded only when infinity and eternity have limits.

Little souls delight in fault-finding; big ones in appreciating. Mean folk are always minus folk; it is the great hearts who are the plus ones. They add to life and make it richer; they call out all that is best within us by the sunshine of their appreciation.

Give attention to life's inflow; outward service will dwindle if inward energies are not renewed.

Much of our spectacular organization in Pentecost is just a splendid emptiness, while some quiet and unobtrusive fellowship is just laden with the excellent glory of the Lord.

We have only touched the outer circle of the great maelstrom of life in the Spirit; there are hidden wonders in the untrodden realm of the divine love; there are new trails to be followed through the tropical luxuriance of redeeming grace.

"Be filled with the Spirit," i. e., Be *crammed* with the Spirit, so filled that there will be no room left for anything else. What is the advantage of such a life? We can only feel what reaches the central realm of consciousness. If we keep evil out of that inner realm, we destroy its virulence. So if we have our consciousness filled with the presence of the glory of the Lord, there will be no room even for the aggressive errors of destructive criticism, or for bitter disappointment.

There is no person ever able to talk about the victory over temptation without he goes through it. All the victories are won in battles.

You must every day make higher ground. You must deny yourself to make progress with God. You must refuse everything that is not pure and holy. God wants you pure in heart. He wants you to have an intense desire after holiness.

It is when we believe that something happens.

The Word of God never profits unless it is mixed with faith in them that hear it.

God wants you so full of the Spirit that your whole life is praise.

The greatest plan that Christ showed forth was the ministry of service. When we come to a place where we serve for pure love's sake, we shall find the hand of the divine Master upon us, and we shall never fail.

You are bound forever by loyalty to God to see that no schism shall come into the body—the church.

Two things will get you to leap out of yourselves into the great promises of God today. One is purity, and the other is faith, which is kindled more and more by purity.

God has no room for the man that looks back, thinks back, or acts back.

The Word of God has not to be prayed about; the Word of God is to be received and obeyed.

There is always blessing where there is harmony. "One accord" is the keynote to victory. See to it that nothing ever comes out of your lips that would disturb harmony, but rather live in the place where you are helping everybody, lifting everybody, and causing everybody to come into perfect harmony.

Be not afraid to ask, for God is on the throne ready to answer.

You can always be down in the dumps when you live by your feelings. Remember that God has raised us up in Christ far above all things. He says, "All things are yours." We are "heirs of God, and joint-heirs with Christ."

* * * * *

One Sunday he was in a strange town, and in his search for a place of worship he found himself in a Friends' Meeting House. He sat quietly just like other people for a time, and then his experience became like that of the psalmist who said, "While I was musing the fire burned: then spake I with my tongue." His soul was ablaze, for he had just left a Salvation Army "knee drill," and liquid fire flowed from his lips. At the close of the service the leaders gathered around him exclaiming, "How quickly you are moved by the Spirit! What is your secret? Do please tell us." They were somewhat astounded at his blunt reply: "Well, you see, it is like this. If the Spirit does not move me, I move the Spirit." That was doubtless a crude way for him to express himself, but we have often heard him say, "As I start out in the natural, in faith, the Spirit of God always meets me and anoints me, so that although I start in the natural I continue in the Spirit."

It could be said of Smith Wigglesworth that he was unique, original and illimitable. He was too sincere to be a mimic and too transparent to be imitated. There were those who sought to borrow his innovations, but they found that these imitations were as incongruous to them as Saul's armor was to David, as useless as Elisha's rod was to Gehazi, and as revealing as was the terrible experience of the seven sons of Sceva who sought to cast out demons in the name of the Christ whom Paul preached.

XII

FREEDOM FROM COVETOUSNESS

~~~~~~~~~~~~~~~~~

"KEEP YOUR life free from love of money, and be content with what you have," is the revised version of Hebrews 13:5. Smith Wigglesworth believed and obeyed this scripture verse as he sought to believe and obey every other word in the Scriptures.

At one time he was the guest of a reputed millionaire in London, and together they took an early morning walk in Hyde Park. Wigglesworth remarked, "Brother, I have not a care in the world. I am as happy as the birds and just as free." Yet at that very moment he had in his pocket letters from home, the contents of which would have filled most men's hearts with fear and anxiety and bowed them down with deep concern.

"What do you say? What do you say? Will you repeat that?" the millionaire asked. He did, and his friend remarked, "I would give all that I possess to be able to say that." If he had given a single hint to that man concerning his great financial needs, he could have had all the money he required. This wealthy man would have esteemed it a privilege to meet all the urgent needs mentioned in those letters. But the approval of God and personal freedom were, in Wigglesworth's opinion, of much greater value than being in financial bondage to any man. "Thou shalt take no gift; for the gift blindeth the wise, and perverteth the word of the righteous," is a scripture he knew by heart. To the end he kept financially clean and could truthfully say, "I have coveted no man's silver or gold." He could lock his lips, seal his heart, and smile through in public, and yet be carrying loads that would break a giant's back. In the presence of God he would unload everything, and storm heaven until the assurance came and all his needs were met.

When any church was seeking to have him for a campaign, one of the terms on which he insisted was that there should be one or more missionary collections. He would not ask anything for himself but he could ask largely of those who were preaching the gospel in the regions beyond. He said to us one time, "I would like to have my picture taken at the time I am writing a missionary check. That is the time when I really look happy."

During one of his campaigns, a check for a considerable sum was put into his hands. He made inquiries about the donor. He was assured that the party who had given this money was wealthy and the gift carried no conditions. He sent the money to a certain missionary association for their use. Later he learned that there were circumstances in the life of the donor that he considered unsatisfactory, and he returned the whole sum in installments as his income allowed.

He hated extravagance and waste. In the years of war, when income was low, expenses high, and the prices of commodities soared, it was always considered prudent to keep from him the price of housekeeping. If he learned that the price of food on the table was, in his estimation, excessive, he would not touch it and invariably it had to be removed from his sight. He could be stingy with himself, but he never was with others, especially where the work of God was concerned. He was

never niggardly in the use of his money, but money had to be his servant and not his master. He would say, "The wise man never spends more than nineteen of his twenty shillings, but the fool spends twenty and thus becomes beggared."

At the close of the last meeting of one of his big campaigns, one for which he had received a very liberal remuneration, he was introduced to two missionaries from China. They had need of a considerable sum to get them to their destination. Learning this, he endorsed the check he had received, the salary for a month's hard work, and handed it to the two men. He did this sort of thing on more than one occasion.

For a number of years he gave all the income from his book *Ever Increasing Faith* to help Christian work and workers in many lands. His mail brought him letters of appeal from all over the world, and if it were in his power to help he never failed to do so.

There were, however, those who abused his generosity. On one occasion, when he was on his way to Australia and New Zealand, he passed through the United States and arrangements were made for American campaigns when he returned. While in New Zealand God wonderfully poured out His Spirit and the whole country was stirred. The revival was at its height when the time for his return to fulfill the promised engagements drew near. He received letters from the people concerned, but he replied that it would be difficult to leave New Zealand at that time. Letters and cables passed between the two countries, but the people to whom he had given the promise were unyielding in their demand that he come to America at the time agreed.

Despite cables, expressing the wish of thousands of New Zealanders, Wigglesworth was compelled to make the three weeks' journey. The church that had asked him for a campaign had promised to pay his return fare and give him a liberal love offering in return for a month's campaign. They asked permission to print and sell his addresses which were taken down stenograph-

ically. Throughout the meetings they made intense appeals and took up special offerings for a new Bible school they were building. During this time the officers of the church approached him and appealed to him to release them from the promise to pay his return fare. He told them that he was in need of the money, and that he had left revival and financial prosperity in New Zealand because they had compelled him. Finally he yielded to their pressure and absolved them from that obligation. The campaign closed and the people testified to great blessings, but the officers of the church failed to fulfil their promises. He left that city a poorer but a much wiser man. For a short while, to avoid a recurrence of like unfair dealing, he sought a clear financial understanding with the assemblies who invited him, but as a rule he found there was no necessity for this.

At one time the pastor of a very large church said to him: "Brother, you have been here three months and your ministry has put this work on a new and solid footing. You cannot leave us. Our people have demanded that we retain you at any price, and the board of this church has asked me to request you to name your figure. You can have anything you want if you will only stay with us." The speaker went on to suggest an astronomical amount if he would only continue his ministry in that church, but Wigglesworth was adamant as he replied: "I have done what God wanted me to do in this place, and now not all the money in the world would be enough to keep me. Gather your church board together and I will pray with you and them, and then say goodbye." A pleading, weeping group of men met him and urged him to reconsider his verdict, but he had made up his mind. He prayed with them and for them and left them saying: "I have a peace no money can buy. I have heaven's smile, and that is worth millions of dollars. I have the divine approval that I would not sacrifice for all the gold in the world. A minute under the unction of God is worth more than worlds. The good will of God

on my head and heart is priceless treasure. Should I sacrifice these for earth's gold? Never!! Never!!!"

Our Greatheart was a friend of many rich people in different parts of the world, yet he was never the slave of any. Had he been covetous, he could have been extremely wealthy, but we have often heard him quote the words of Elisha, "Is it a time to receive money?"

Offers such as the following came to him. A millionaire brewer, who had tried the world's best specialists for his sick wife, without avail, urged him to spare neither time nor money to come at once to aid her. Parents whose children were mentally afflicted were ready to pay any price for their deliverance. Rich, dissipated, physically ruined people sought his aid. They cabled and wrote him, "Come; fly over; money no object." He gave a deaf ear to all these financial offers. He would not move out of the will of God. If being pure meant being poor, he was quite willing for that.

While he knew the value and the need of money, he knew, too, its snare. In planning his itineraries and acknowledging offers for campaigns in different churches, the financial remuneration was never the deciding factor. Prospects could be elusive and promises could break down. These things he knew from bitter experience. But he had proved that by putting God first, all the resources of God were at his disposal.

He always bore that scripture in mind, "To do good and to communicate forget not: for with such sacrifices God is well pleased." When he was visiting the city of Springfield, Missouri, in 1923, he stayed in the writer's home. At that time my wife and I were not overburdened with filthy lucre. He must have noticed that we were somewhat shabbily dressed, our income being small in those days, for he took us downtown and purchased a new suit and hat for me and a new outfit for my wife. He was just overwhelmed with joy at being able to perform this kindness to two people whom he loved, and I remember that in one of the stores, like Joseph, "he sought where to weep." He went into one dark corner of the store where he hoped no clerk could see him, and there he wiped away the copious tears that were falling from his eyes.

He used every opportunity to induce people to be generous in their giving to God's work. Standing before a crowded audience in a large auditorium in London during a Pentecostal convention, he announced, "This is my birthday. I am seventy today. Now I know that many of you people love me and that you would like to give me a birthday present. Some of you ladies have come to stay in this city for a few days. You possess more dresses and hats than you need, and they will last you a long time. And you men, too, can make your clothes last a bit longer. You all can save money, and give it as a birthday offering to God. We will use the offering for missionary work throughtout the world." The audience smilingly rose to the occasion and gave a record offering. It was a timely blessing to the work of God overseas. To Wigglesworth, giving was always more blessed than receiving, and he preached and practiced the art of laying up treasures in heaven.

After his homegoing, a friend in Melbourne, Australia, wrote: "I can never forget the first convention in Sunderland, in 1908. A collection was taken for foreign missionaries. The amount received was about seventy pounds (about $350.00 in those days). When the total was announced there was some handclapping. But Wigglesworth was disappointed at so small an offering and he arose, with tears running down his face, and said reprovingly, 'Pentecost and seventy pounds!' About twenty-six years ago I was at his convention in Bradford and the missionary collection was about 1,200 pounds ($6,000.00). The next year he got 1,350 pounds ($6,750.00)."

XIII

A GREAT FIGHT OF FAITH

IN 2 Samuel 23:8-12 we read short summaries of the exploits of three of David's mighty men of valor. Adino lifted up his spear against eight hundred foes whom he slew at one time. Eleazar defied the Philistines; he smote them until his hand was weary, and his hand clave unto his sword. This resulted in a great victory and much spoil for Israel. Shammah stood in the midst of a ground full of Gentiles, and defended it. As a result of his gallant stand, the attacking Philistines were slain and the Lord wrought a great victory. It was on a similar line to that of these three heroes that our Greatheart fought a good fight of faith.

To the almost universal question, "How can we have great faith?" he would reply: "Great faith is the product of great fights. Great testimonies are the outcome of great tests. Great triumphs can only come out of great trials." It is significant that the highest military decorations in many countries are symbolized by a cross—that sign of greatest conflict and greatest victory.

There are many who contest the truth that Christ

heals the sick today, but our Greatheart based his preaching and practicing on the truth that Christ is still the same, and that the Lord who changes not still says to every sick and needy one, "I am the Lord that healeth thee." One of his great friends, Thomas Myerscough, was responsible for the statement," He that has an experience is not at the mercy of a man who merely has an argument." Our Greatheart had a rocklike background in his own personal experience of the Lord's healing, and he saw healing flow out from the Lord to thousands to whom he ministered. The Lord let him go through many testings and trials in his experience, but he would frequently testify: "God has repeatedly sent His steamroller over me and flattened me out; but He has never left me on the ground." Earlier in this book we have told how God healed him of appendicitis when a zealous young man jumped on his body, dug his fist deeply into the pit of his stomach, as he battled through in prayer and obtained deliverance and healing for the dying man.

We have also told of his deliverance from a long and serious condition of hemorrhoids or what is frequently termed bleeding piles. The scripture that the Lord gave him on this occasion was: "From the days of John the Baptist until now the kingdom of heaven suffereth violence, and the violent take it by force." He interpreted this as a call to the exercise of violent or forceful faith on his part in order to overcome this trial in his body. At that time he literally stormed the throne of grace and took the kingdom by force. In later days, his prayer for the demon oppressed was characterized by holy violence, and he sought to fulfill the fast of Isaiah 58, "to loose the bands of wickedness, to undo the heavy burdens, and to let the oppressed go free." His attitude was never that of a child stroking a kitten, but rather of one who tore the prey out of the mouth of the dragon.

In the latter part of his life he had three tremendous physical tests. The first of these commenced about fifteen years before his homegoing, and it was a record of miraculous faith and fortitude on his part. He went to a doctor whom he knew, who said to him, "Mr. Wigglesworth, I have received the X-ray plates which show your condition, and the report is a very serious one. They reveal kidney stones in an advanced stage. If you will take my advice, you will submit to an operation at the earliest possible opportunity. It is the only thing that can save you from a prolonged and painful illness, and eventually these stones will kill you. Let me telephone to the hospital and get a bed for you immediately."

Looking up into the eager face of the doctor, he said, "Doctor, the God who made this body is the one who can cure it. No knife shall ever cut it so long as I live." "What about these stones?" asked the doctor. "God will deal with them," was the answer. The doctor said, "Well, if ever He does, I shall be interested to know about it." "You shall," answered Mr. Wigglesworth as he left the office.

The pains increased and night and day there was local irritation. A vessel was placed for his use in a convenient place in his home. After an unusually trying day, his daughter went to empty this vessel and noticed a thick grey sediment at the bottom. In it was a substance like the shell of a nut, rough edged and brittle. To pass such a thing in kidney action must have caused excruciating pain. When he was shown this he remarked, "This is the beginning of the end. The Lord has operated." It was the beginning, but the end was a long way off. There were to be many years of agony before he passed the last stone. He showed the doctor what had come from him and the doctor had to admit that it was a miracle that he had been able to eject such a thing from the kidneys. How he endured such incessant torture, with every nerve dancing with pain when he passed large quantities of blood as he struggled to eject the stones, and yet continued his ministry without any intermission, was an astounding thing to those who knew of his battle.

One day he arose from his bed to take a journey to

the Isle of Man, which was quite a distance from his home, to pray for some sick people. This meant a three hours' railroad journey before he boarded the ocean-going boat with its trying sea passage of some hours in wintry weather. On his arrival a relative (who was a nurse) met him and pleaded with him to go to bed with hot water bottles, etc., because he was so ill. But he stayed on the island until he had ministered healing and deliverance to the sick ones. He struggled with moving stones on the outward and return journey and passed so much blood that his cheeks were blanched, and he had to be wrapped in heavy rugs to give him warmth.

Later, accompanied by his son-in-law, he went to Sweden and Norway for a protracted visit. All night long he was in and out of bed as he struggled to emit stones, rolling on the floor in agony. Yet he would rise and minister to the sick twice each day. In the large Filadelfia Church in Stockholm, the ministry to the sick was unusually heavy. At the close of one day the pastor, Lewi Pethrus, said there were about eight hundred in the night service. Miracles of healing were wrought as he ministered to the people in the name of the Lord Jesus Christ, yet he was more sick than the people he prayed for, and he received no relief for himself. It could truthfully be said that "he ministered in the infirmity of the flesh."

In Switzerland he passed through the churches like a flame. Revival followed his ministry. Souls were saved, bodies were healed of all kinds of diseases; the big halls were filled, and the people were blessed. Very few people knew that he was going through the biggest test of his life; he towered above it all like a rock.

When in America he filled the biggest halls, ministered to record crowds, prayed for thousands of people, and yet the trial continued. Frequently his son-in-law and daughter had to leave him in bed. After they had begun the meeting, he would rise and go to the church, preach and pray for the sick, and then return to his bed. At times, in the meeting, he would bear the agony he was suffering as long as he could, and then run off the platform and seek a place of relief, only to return and carry on the service.

James Salter testifies: "Living with him, sharing his bedroom as we frequently did during those years, we marveled at the unquenched zeal in his fiery preaching and his compassionate ministry to the sick. I do not remember his ever absenting himself from any meeting during that period, although there were times when he had to leave the preaching to others. Knowing him as perhaps no other man did, being together under the most intimate conditions, sharing mutual secrets, having every opportunity to weigh and assess him physically and spiritually, one cannot find the answer to the struggle of those days and years in the iron constitution and will of steel, both of which he possessed; for I have seen those things break down under lesser tests. He did not just bear those agonies; he made them serve the purpose of God and gloried in and over them.

"He had a glass bottle in which he kept many of the stones he had passed, and finally there were some hundreds of them. After a test of at least six years he emerged with his fire-tried faith firmer than ever, and a renewed and unshakable trust in his God. He aspired to be like Job—someone in whom God would glory over the devil. Throughout the whole period of his trial, his confidence was expressed in the words of Job: 'But He knoweth the way that I take: when He hath tried me, I shall come forth as gold. My foot hath held His steps, His way have I kept and not declined.'"

In 1937 our Greatheart visited South Africa. He frequently remarked that it was the most trying tour he ever made in his life. He was not well when he left England and he boarded the ship in great pain. For the major part of the voyage he suffered intensely with sciatica which at times locked his legs and made walking extremely painful. Despite this drawback his early campaigns were richly blessed of God and the results of his soul-saving and body-healing ministry are standing today.

A man who had derived great benefits from reading his book, *Ever Increasing Faith,* purchased a roomy automobile and undertook to drive him all the time he was in South Africa. In many ways this was a great blessing. In some other respects it had its drawbacks. His daughter was with him on this trip, and his son-in-law journeyed down from the Belgian Congo and traveled with him for a few weeks.

One night, after an exceptionally heavy service, Mr. Salter was helping him to bed, when he locked the bedroom door and revealed that he had been ruptured badly. He said it was due to getting in and out of the automobile. That may have climaxed it, but he had been jumping off some high platforms during his preaching and healing services and for a man of seventy-eight this practice was doubtless dangerous. But he completed his tour, his disability known only to his son-in-law and daughter.

Speaking of that tour, Mr. Salter says: "How he worked and preached! There were meetings in large halls and he traveled thousands of miles over corrugated dirt roads, preaching and praying for the sick, both black and white, eating unusual food, perspiring in the hot sun, and yet he never spared himself. He certainly did not behave like a badly ruptured man. It was another of the secrets that God and he shared and overcame."

In the autumn of 1944 he had another severe period of physical testing. At that time he was eighty-five years of age. As was his custom he had been sitting in the park at the end of the road near where he lived. But when he came home at midday it was noticed that his face was twisted and that he had little use of one side of his body. He smiled, but his speech was affected. He was given some food and his loved ones put him to bed. The rest of the day he was semi-conscious. When nighttime came his son felt that a doctor ought to see him.

The doctor, who had advised an operation on the previous occasion, examined him. But he pleaded with the doctor, "Please leave me alone." The doctor thought it was resentment, but he was really so sick that he did not know what he was saying and he did not even recognize the doctor. The doctor diagnosed the case and told the members of the family, "He has had a sunstroke. Keep him in bed for a day or two." The doctor drew Mr. Salter aside and said, "He may not get over this; he can go any time. He may pass in his sleep." After a day or two in bed, he was able to get up, and the first thing he did was to go over to the doctor and apologize, explaining to him that he had not known what he was doing or saying. But he had been badly shaken and was unsteady in hands and feet. In fact, he had one or two bad falls.

His loved ones cared for him all the winter, but early in the following year he had a miraculous touch in mind and body. He began to write all his own letters and went about as usual. God quickened Romans 8:11 to him: "But if the Spirit of Him that raised up Jesus from the dead dwell in you, He that raised up Christ from the dead shall also quicken your mortal bodies by His Spirit that dwelleth in you." His speech and letters were full of this message. He was entirely rejuvenated and wrote the story of his healing for publication. When Easter came around he took his usual place as Chairman of the Preston Convention, which was always one of the outstanding Easter meetings in England. He could scarcely wait until the first few songs were sung in the opening service before he began to give his testimony. Romans 8:11 was his text and topic all through the series of meetings, and his witness to this new life vitalized every service throughout the whole convention. Again we heard his old familiar expression, "Why, I don't know that I have a body!" In this state of spiritual and physical glow he continued until the day of his homegoing.

XIV

A LIFE OF JOY

SMITH WIGGLESWORTH often said: "No man gets more out of life than I do. I get more out of a minute than most folks get out of a month."

He reminded us of a grown-up schoolboy in his simple delights. He loved to roam the woodlands. He knew all the birds of his native land and their songs. One day his elder son said to him, "Father, we have found a young cuckoo in a titlark's nest. It is just by the roadside." Immediately he desired to drive out and see it. How fascinated he was as he watched the fledgling, in its tiny nest, open its mouth each time it heard a sound. It illustrated to him the scripture text, "Open thy mouth wide, and I will fill it." Psalm 81:10.

He reveled in the violets, the primroses, the bluebells, and the heather of his native land. James Salter tells of spending a day with him in the country: "After ascending a long grade we emerged into a wonderful stretch of moorland—miles and miles of it. As far as the eye could see, the ground was carpeted with a gorgeous covering of purple heather, just at its fullest and best.

The sun shone brilliantly, the birds soared and sang, all nature seemed to be reveling in a holiday mood. The air was like balm, and Smith Wigglesworth raised his arms in his characteristic way, threw back his shoulders, and began to breathe in deeply as he exclaimed 'This is wine, this is health, this is life!' An elderly man who was passing, stopped and looked at these extravagant actions; and when Mr. Wigglesworth saw him, he addressed him saying, 'What a wonderful place to live in this must be. Surely, people never die here!' He much enjoyed the answer of the old man, who said, with a twinkle in his eye, 'Only once, Mister; only once!'

"Flowing water was like a soothing song to him. 'I would like to spend a night in that bedroom overlooking this babbling stream,' he would say. He was a boy again as he sat on the bank of a lovely stream, watching a country boy catching trout and lifting them out of the water for him to see. He soared and sang with the larks and the linnets, and he romped with the young rabbits.

"His holidays were holy days. He relaxed, but he never retired from the work he loved so well—the work of bringing souls to Christ. While they were both young, he and his wife went on a cycling tour in Scotland. In one of the towns through which they passed, an open-air gospel service was in progress. An open-air meeting was always a joy to Mrs. Wigglesworth, so she entered the ring and spoke for a short time. The Provost of the town heard her, and learning that she was an evangelist, he immediately arranged a week's special meetings for her. The nights were spent in a blessed series of soul-saving services. In the daytime Smith Wigglesworth took the opportunity to climb one of Scotland's highest mountains, and on the mountainside he was able to lead three men to the Lord before he returned home.

"He always had a special liking for North Wales. Even when he was well advanced in years, it was a joy to walk to the summit of Mount Snowdon and down again—which is quite a feat for younger folk, for that is the highest mountain in the British Isles. How he delighted to see the sun rise from such an elevation. On one occasion he and his daughter arranged to have a cycling holiday in North Wales. It was in the day of the Welsh revival in 1905. One day, following the crowd which was too big for any building, they entered a large field. There was no visible leader in the meeting but God's Spirit was present. The singing of hymns and choruses mingled with the prayers; everybody seemed lost in the thought of expressing their heart's emotion in some suitable way. There was no start and no stop, and the meetings appeared to continue indefinitely.

"Smith Wigglesworth enjoyed the holy atmosphere of the meeting, but after awhile he said to his daughter, 'Let us go for a bite of food. We will follow this path; it will lead us somewhere.' The pathway led to a farmyard where a woman was very busy. 'We have some food here with us; could you make us something to drink?' asked Mr. Wigglesworth. 'Why, of course,' she replied. 'But you must excuse my appearance,' she explained, 'we are only doing what is absolutely necessary these days, as we are spending all the time we can at the revival. Of course, we have to milk and feed the cows, and attend to the hens. We are not bothering much about food.' She began to get some tea for them to drink.

"'Are you saved?' Mr. Wigglesworth asked her. 'Well, no; not in the way that Evan Roberts says we should be. We are Methodists.' 'Well,' he replied, 'you can be saved—saved in the only way that people can be saved, and that is through faith in the Lord Jesus Christ.' Opening his New Testament at Romans 10:9, he read to the woman: 'If thou shalt confess with thy mouth the Lord Jesus, and shalt believe in thine heart that God hath raised him from the dead, thou shalt be saved.' 'That is how people get saved and become born again,' he explained. He had the pleasure of leading that woman to the Lord Jesus. Leaving North Wales by boat for Liverpool, he and his daughter had the joy of pointing two men to their Savior."

When in California it was always his joy to visit the Yosemite Valley. Every night a huge bonfire is made, and every night at nine o'clock, exactly, a voice calls out: "Let the fire fall." Then from a rock about a thousand feet high, blazing timbers are thrust over the side and the fire falls like a flaming waterfall. Said Mr. Salter: "It was at such a scene witnessed by thousands of people that we heard him give forth one of his loudest 'Hallelujahs.' What an echo sounded through the valley, and what a shock it gave to the audience! Such a sight of falling fire stirred his Pentecostal soul to the depths, and he never forgot that scene.

"Another occasion that lives in our memory was when we had listened to Handel's masterpiece, *The Messiah.* The oratorio was climaxed with the Hallelujah Chorus, which brought the audience to its feet, and as the choir closed its last note he lifted his voice in an ecstatic 'Hallelujah' that filled the hall and made the rafters ring. A reporter, writing up the event for the next day's paper, made the comment: 'I never heard such a voice in my life!'

"His pleasure in persons, in places, and in pictures was unbounded. When traveling through different countries he always availed himself of the opportunity to see the principal sights. There were two things he saw that always had great spiritual inspiration for him. One was Niagara Falls, and the other the Trummelbach Falls in Switzerland. Looking at these two majestic, rushing torrents, he would plead, with the tears streaming from his eyes: *'Like that,* my God, *like that in me!* Out of my innermost being let there flow, *like that,* vast, fast rivers of living water.' Usually after visiting Niagara he would go to New York City for his final American campaign, and invariably he would urge his audiences to receive a *'like that'* experience.

"The sight of these masterpieces of nature affected him like the minstrel's art affected Elisha—they set his soul aglow and his spirit ablaze in the incense of prayer and praise, and I have seen him dance in a spirit of abandonment. Then his hands would rise spontaneously in worship and he would indulge in an exhibition of jubilation that was contagious. With tears streaming down his cheeks he would invariably say, 'Brethren, let's pray.' He would turn every place into a Bethel and every group of people into worshipers of the living God.

"His joy continued to the end and he would say, 'I have no regrets, and there is nothing for which I wish to turn back.' When Christmas or his birthday came around, the people would ask him what kind of present he would like, and he would reply: 'There's not a single thing in this world that I want. I have all I need.'

"He completed the full circle of a Christian ministry, omitted no known item on the program, lived ablaze for God, igniting other lives, and moved under divine pressure to enter heaven like a fully laden ship entering into port. He 'finished his course.'

"How jealously he guarded the faith he preached and practiced. He thought that it was better to die trusting than to live doubting. A testimony of healing in which God, doctors, operations and medicines shared the credit always failed to find his full approval. His was the spirit of the Holy Mount, where, when three tabernacles were mentioned, two persons were withdrawn and a voice came out of the cloud, saying: 'This is My beloved Son . . . hear ye Him.' And suddenly, when they looked round about, they saw no one save Jesus only, and themselves.

"He was intensely zealous that God alone should have all the glory. No mountain was big enough and no circumstance was wide enough to allow another person, if Jesus was on it or in it.

"To him, keeping the faith in its integrity, and living under the sunshine of God's approving smile, meant to have the attitude of Job, who said, 'Though He slay me, yet will I trust in Him;' and the attitude of the three Hebrews who said to Nebuchadenezzar, 'We are not careful to answer thee in this matter. If it be so, our God whom we serve is able to deliver us from the burning fiery furnace, and He will deliver us out of thine hand, O king. But if not, be it known unto thee, O king, that we will not serve thy gods, nor worship the golden image which thou hast set up.' To them, burning was preferable to bending. One of his slogans was, 'If you would be crowned with righteousness, keep the faith.' "

There were two great sorrows in his life. One was the homegoing of his dear wife in 1913. Mrs. Wigglesworth served the Lord until the very last moment of her life. It was as she was returning from Bowland Street Mission that her heart failed her. That night Mr. Wigglesworth was going to Scotland, but news reached him at the station before he boarded the train that his wife was very sick. He rushed home. We gather from what he has told us, that her spirit had already departed to be with the Lord, but when he rebuked death her spirit came back for just a short while. But then the Lord spoke to his heart and told him, "This is the time that I want to take her home to Myself." And so with a breaking heart he released the one he had loved for so many years to go to be with Christ. But it seemed to us that from that moment his ministry took on a new sweetness and a new power.

In the year 1915, his youngest son George went to be with the Lord. This was a great wound to his loving heart, but from the letters that followed, after his boy's homegoing, it seemed as though the father again entered into a deeper consecration and a new and larger and yet more sympathetic ministry for his Lord and Master.

XV

THE FULL CORN IN THE EAR

~~~~~~~~~~~~~~~~~~~~~~~~~~~~~~~

WELL! AND how is she?" How often our Greatheart had asked such a question. These words were typical of his loving heart, revealing itself in oneness with human frailties and in compassionate sympathy with those who suffered pain. But this was the last time he asked it, and these were the last words Smith Wigglesworth ever spoke on this earth.

Some weeks previously, he had visited the house of a very sick woman in Wakefield. For years she had suffered the intense ravages of cancer throughout her body and had endured excruciating pain. From the natural viewpoint her case was hopeless. As he ministered the Word to this dear woman and prayed for her, she responded to his ministry. The power of God was mightily manifested, and she arose from her bed and walked around the room with her hands uplifted. It surely appeared as though God had healed her. Our Greatheart had been greatly blessed in his own spirit when praying for this sister, and when he returned to Bradford his daughter wrote: "The house was filled with the presence and fragrance of God. The worship was lovely. He prayed, 'O Lord, Thou knowest that we have never turned from Thy Word for a moment. Thy Word has always been sufficient. Thou knowest, Lord, we have never doubted Thy Word. Thou art the Healer, the Deliverer, and all we need.' It was a lovely, simple, childlike prayer, and it was heaven to see his countenance."

Some little while after the above incident, he went to see this woman's pastor, Wilfred Richardson, who had been hurried to a hospital and had undergone what was thought to be an absolutely necessary operation. Tears of sympathy and love blended as these two elderly men affectionately embraced each other. "What will they say?" exclaimed the sick man. "What can I tell my people? I who have preached divine healing for over thirty years am now in the hospital and have submitted to an operation!"

Despite the loving counsel and comfort of his friend, this pastor continued to reproach himself, saying: "I can never forgive myself, never!" Possibly this attitude of heart contributed to his death, which took place about ten weeks later.

The winter months had been exceptionally severe, much snow had fallen, and so Smith Wigglesworth, who was now eighty-seven years of age, was indoors a good deal. However, when he heard of the death of this dear friend, he said, "I must attend his funeral."

He dressed in a warm suit, and remarked how wonderfully well he felt. Some friends took him to Wakefield in their car, and they said they had never seen him so jubilant. As they journeyed the thirteen miles, he pointed out to them the various churches in which he and his wife had conducted revival services, and told of incidents connected with these meetings. James Salter had been asked to conduct the funeral service, and he arrived at the church building ahead of his father-in-law. When Wigglesworth came, Salter invited him into the vestry where a small fire of coal was burning.

As he entered the door, he met Mr. Hibbert, the father of the sick woman for whom he had prayed for deliverance from cancer. It was to this dear man of God that the question was addressed: "Well! And how is she?"

He awaited the reply with an eagerness almost bordering on impatience. He expected to hear that she was completely delivered, but the answer came in a hesitant manner: "She is a little better, a bit easier; her pains have not been quite so bad during the past few days." This was not the victorious report he had expected, and the anguish of his pent-up disappointment found expression in a body-convulsing sigh that came from the depth of his being. It was that sigh of compassion that broke the heart of Smith Wigglesworth. His chin fell on his chest. Without any pain whatever he went to be with the Lord he loved so well and whom he had served so faithfully from his childhood days. He had written to us a few weeks previously about Enoch's walking with God and walking right into the glory. He was constantly praying that he might indeed be an Enoch; and he was. His sudden homegoing was very much like a translation. He was not; for God took him.

Some fifteen years previously, according to a friend, he had said at a convention, "I am asking the Lord for fifteen more years of life and service." The Lord gave him those fifteen years, even down to the very week. During those years he visited most of the countries in Europe, besides the United States and South Africa; and he had the joy of seeing the Word confirmed with signs following, to the glory of God.

Sometimes when he was past eighty years it would be said to him, "I wonder who will receive your mantle." He would reply, "I am not done with it yet!" But as he would tell his audiences all over the world, "God has everything for you. He does not want you to come behind in any gift. The one thing He calls upon you to do is to *believe* Him." He would say, "I can get more out of God by believing Him for one minute than by shouting at Him all night." "If you will open your heart to

God's grace, God will come in and place in you definite faith." All round the world his faith was expressed in the simple song:

> *"Only believe, only believe;*
> *All things are possible, only believe."*

XVI

YET SPEAKING

~~~~~~~~~~~~~~~~~~~~~~~~~~

WE CLOSE this volume with one of Smith Wigglesworth's sermons on the theme of Faith.

A Sermon on Faith by Smith Wigglesworth

"By *faith* Abel offered unto God a more excellent sacrifice than Cain . . . *by faith* Enoch was translated that he should not see death . . . *by faith* Noah . . . prepared an ark to the saving of his house . . . *by faith* Abraham, when he was called to go out into a place which he should after receive for an inheritance, obeyed" (Hebrews 11:4-8). There is only one way to all the treasures of God, and that is *the way of faith*. All things are possible; the fulfilling of all promises is *to him that believeth*.

When the word came to Zacharias, he was filled with unbelief until the angel said, "Thou shalt be dumb . . . because thou believest not my words" (Luke 1:20). Mary said, "Be it unto me according to thy word"

(Luke 1:38). And the Lord was pleased that she believed that there would be a performance. When we believe what God has said, *there shall be a performance.*

There were people praying all night that Peter might come out of prison. But there seemed to be one thing missing despite all their praying, and that was faith. Rhoda had more faith than all the rest of them. When the knock came at the door, she ran to it, for she was expecting an answer to her prayers; and the moment she heard Peter's voice, she ran back and announced to them that Peter was standing at the door. And all the people said, "You are mad. It isn't so." That was not faith. When she insisted that he was there, they said, "Well, perhaps God has sent his angel." But Rhoda insisted, "It is Peter." And Peter continued knocking. And they went out and found it so. What Rhoda had believed for had become a glorious fact.

Beloved, we may do much praying and groaning, but we do not receive from God because of that; we receive because we believe. But when a man labors in prayer, he groans and travails because his tremendous sin is weighing him down, and he becomes broken in the presence of God; and when properly melted he comes into perfect harmony with the divine plan of God, and then God can work in that clay. He could not before. Prayer changes hearts, but it never changes God. He is the same yesterday, and today, and for ever—full of love, full of compassion, full of mercy, full of grace, and ready to bestow this and communicate that to us as we come in faith to Him.

Believe that when you come into the presence of God you can have all you came for. You can take it away, and you can use it, for all the power of God is at your disposal in response to your faith. The price for all was paid by the blood of Jesus Christ at Calvary.

We read in Hebrews 11:5, "By faith Enoch was translated that he should not see death . . . before his translation he had this testimony, that he pleased God." We are called to walk together with God through the

Spirit. It is delightful to know that we can talk with God and hold communion with Him. Through this wonderful baptism in the Spirit which the Lord gives us, He enables us to talk to Himself in a language that the Spirit has given, a language which no man understands, but which He understands, a language of love. Oh, how wonderful it is to speak to Him in the Spirit, to let the Spirit lift, and lift and lift us until He takes us into the very presence of God! I pray that God by His Spirit may move all of us so that we walk with God, even as Enoch walked with Him. But beloved, it is a walk by faith and not by sight, a walk of believing the Word of God.

I want to show you the difference between our faith and the faith of Jesus. Our faith is limited and comes to an end. Most people have experienced coming to the place where they have said, "Lord, I can go no further. I have gone so far, and I cannot go on." But God can help us and take us beyond this. I remember one night, being in the north of England. I was taken into a house where there was a young woman lying on her bed, a very helpless case. Her reason was gone and many things were manifested that were absolutely satanic.

She was a beautiful young woman. Her husband was quite a young man. He came in with a baby in his arms, leaned over and kissed his wife. The moment he did so she threw herself over on the other side of the bed, just as a lunatic would do, with no consciousness of the presence of her husband. It was heartbreaking. The husband took the baby and pressed the baby's lips to the mother. Again there was a wild frenzy. I said to the sister who was attending her, "Have you anybody to help?" She answered, "We have done everything we could." I said, "Have you no spiritual help?" Her husband stormed and said, "Spiritual help? Do you think we believe in God after we have had seven weeks of no sleep and this maniac condition? If you think we believe in God, you are mistaken. You have come to the wrong house."

There was a young woman about eighteen who grinned at me as she passed out of the door, as much as to say, "You cannot do anything." But this brought me to a place of compassion for this poor young woman. And then with what faith I had I began to penetrate the heavens. I was soon out on the heights. And I tell you I have never seen a man get anything from God who prayed on the earth level. If you get anything from God you will have to pray right into heaven, for all you want is there. If you are living an earthly life, all taken up with sensual things, and expect things from heaven, they will never come. God wants us to be a heavenly people, seated with Him in the heavenlies, and laying hold of all the things in heaven that are at our disposal.

I saw there, in the presence of that demented girl, limitations to my faith; but as I prayed there came another faith into my heart that could not be denied, a faith that grasped the promises, a faith that believed God's Word. I came from the presence of the glory back to earth. I was not the same man. I confronted the same conditions I had seen before, but this time it was in the name of Jesus. With a faith that could shake hell and move anything else, I cried to the demon power that was making this young woman a maniac, "Come out of her, in the name of Jesus!" She rolled over and fell asleep, and awakened in fourteen hours, perfectly sane and perfectly whole.

Enoch conversed with God. I want to live in constant conversation with God. I am so grateful that from my youth up, God has given me a relish for the Bible. I find the Bible food for my soul. It is strength to the believer. It builds up our character in God. And as we receive with meekness the Word of God, we are being changed by the Spirit from glory to glory. And by this Book comes faith, for faith cometh by hearing, and hearing by the Word of God.

I believe that all our failures come because of an imperfect understanding of God's Word. I see that it is impossible to please God on any other line but by faith, and everything that is not of faith is sin. You say, "How can I obtain this faith?" You see the secret in Hebrews 12:2, *"Looking unto Jesus the author and finisher of our faith."* He is the author of faith. Oh, the might of our Christ who created the universe and upholds it all by the might of His power! He who made this vast universe will make us a new creation. He spoke the word and the stars came into being; can He not speak the word that will produce a mighty faith in us? Ah, this One who is the author and finisher of our faith comes and dwells within us, quickens us by His Spirit, and molds us by His will. And he who has begun a good work within us will complete it and perfect it, for He not only is the author but the finisher and perfecter of our faith.

"The Word of God is quick and powerful, and sharper than any twoedged sword, piercing even to the dividing asunder of soul and spirit, and of the joints and marrow, and is a discerner of the thoughts and intents of the heart" (Hebrews 4:12). How the Word of God severs the soul and the spirit—the soul which has a lot of carnality, a lot of selfishness in it, a lot of evil in it! Thank God, the Lord can sever from us all that is earthly and sensual, and make us spiritual people. He can bring all our selfishness to the place of death and bring the life of Jesus into our being to take the place of that earthly and sensual thing that is destroyed by the living Word.

The living Word pierces right to the very marrow. When I was in Australia, so many people came to me with double curvature of the spine; but the word of the Lord came right down to the very marrow of their spines, and instantly they were healed and made straight as I laid hands on them in the name of Jesus. The divine Son of God, the living Word, through His power, moved upon those curvatures of the spine and straightened them out. Oh, thank God for the mighty power of the Word!

God has come to lead us out of ourselves into Himself, and to take us from the ordinary into the extraordinary, from the human into the divine, and make us after the image of His Son. Oh, what a Savior! It is written, "Now are we the sons of God, and it doth not yet appear what we shall be: but we know that, when he shall appear, we shall be like him; for we shall see him as he is" (1 John 3:2). But even now, the Lord wants to transform us from glory to glory, by the Spirit of the living God. Have faith in God, have faith in the Son, have faith in the Holy Spirit; and the Triune God will work in you, working in you to will and to do all the good pleasure of His will.

More great works by
Smith Wigglesworth

Ever Increasing Faith

Even for giants of faith, life wasn't worry-free. Wigglesworth shares about his own personal struggles—and triumphs—he experienced even as he led thousands to salvation. This book features a collection of 18 messages, filled with real-life stories, Wigglesworth preached, including: Have Faith in God, Our Risen Christ, Life in the Spirit, The Gift of Prophecy, The Gift of Tongues, Wilt Thou Be Made Whole, and 12 more. Paper.   **02LM0494**

ISBN 0-88243-494-2

Faith That Prevails

Wigglesworth's timeless message tells how God's power is real for today. This faith-building book features numerous stories of personal experiences of salvation, physical healing, and the baptism in the Holy Spirit. Each chapter begins with a Bible reading, then moves on to in-depth discussion. Chapters include: God-given Faith, Life Precious Faith, Spiritual Power, Paul's Pentecost, Ye Shall Receive Power, Keeping the Vision, and Present-time Blessing. Paper.   **02LM0711**

ISBN 0-88243-711-9

To check on pricing information or to order these two Wigglesworth books, contact your local bookstore or call 1-800-641-4310. You may also write:

Gospel Publishing House
1445 Boonville Avenue
Springfield, MO 65802-1894

Postage, handling, and applicable sales tax will be added.